INSIGHT GUIDES

MELBOURNE

Step by Step

D1375448

APA PUBLICATIONS L

Part of the Langenscheidt Publishing Group

THE CITY OF ST KILDA

MCMXCIII

PIONEER WOMENS MEM. GDN.

ABORIGINAL REBURIAL

VICTORIA ARTS
ROYAL BOTANIC GARDENS

ING GEORGE V MON.

MYER MUSIC BOWL

CONTENTS

ABOUT THIS BOOK

Above: *The Public Purse* in Bourke Street; the place to meet friends in Melbourne is under the clocks at Flinders Street Station; Albert Park and the city skyline; view from Eureka Tower on the Southbank; Yarra Valley vineyard.

This *Step by Step Guide* has been produced by the editors of Insight Guides, whose books have set the standard for visual travel guides since 1970. With top-quality photography and authoritative recommendations, this guidebook brings you the very best of Melbourne in a series of 14 tailor-made tours.

WALKS AND TOURS

The tours in the book provide something to suit all budgets, tastes and trip lengths. As well as covering Melbourne's many highlight attractions, the routes track lesser-known sights and up-and-coming areas; there are also excursions for those who want to extend their visit outside the city. The tours embrace a range of interests, so whether you are an art fan or an architecture buff, a gourmet or a barfly, a lover of flora or a follower of fashion, you will find an option to suit.

We recommend that you read the whole of a tour before setting out. This should help you to familiarise yourself with the route and enable you to plan where to stop for refreshments – options for this are shown in the

'Food and Drink' boxes, recognisable by the knife-and-fork sign, on most pages.

For our pick of the walks by theme, consult Recommended Tours For… *(see pp.6–7)*.

OVERVIEW

The tours are set in context by this introductory section, giving an overview of the city to set the scene, plus background information on food and drink, shopping, entertainment and sporting events. A succinct history timeline highlights the key events that have shaped Melbourne over the years.

DIRECTORY

Also supporting the tours is a Directory chapter, comprising a user-friendly, clearly organised A–Z of practical information, our pick of where to stay while you are in the city and select restaurant listings; these eateries complement the more low-key cafés and restaurants that feature within the tours and are intended to offer a wider choice for evening dining. Also included here are some nightlife listings.

The Author

Virginia Maxwell was born and bred in suburban Melbourne. She now lives in the inner city with her partner Peter and young son Max, and with them has visited every corner of Victoria. Virginia has worked as an architectural journalist, museum curator, festival director and book editor, but these days she spends most of her time writing guidebooks and travel articles for a host of international publishers. The things she loves most about her hometown are its vibrant café culture, exciting contemporary architecture and wonderful bookshops.

Margin Tips
Shopping tips, historical facts, handy hints and information on activities help visitors to make the most of their time in Melbourne.

Feature Boxes
Notable topics are highlighted in these special boxes.

Key Facts Box
This box gives details of the distance covered on the tour, plus an estimate of how long it should take. It also states where the route starts and finishes, and gives key travel information such as which days are best to do the route or handy transport tips.

Route Map
Detailed cartography shows the tour clearly plotted with numbered dots. For more detailed mapping, see the pull-out map slotted inside the back cover.

Food and Drink
Recommendations of where to stop for refreshment are given in these boxes. The numbers prior to each restaurant/café name link to references in the main text. Restaurants in the Food and Drink boxes are plotted on the maps.

The $ signs at the end of each entry reflect the approximate cost of a two-course dinner for one with a glass of house wine. These should be seen as a guide only. Price ranges, also quoted on the inside back flap for easy reference, are:

$$$$	over A$80
$$$	A$60–80
$$	A$45–60
$	below A$45

Footers
Look here for the tour name, a map reference and the main attraction on the double-page.

BARFLIES

Of all the gin joints in all the towns in all the world... Melbourne has one of the best selections. Head for Bogey and Bergman on Brunswick Street (walk 5), Fitzroy Street in St Kilda (walk 11), the laneways off Collins Street (walk 1), Bourke Street (walk 2) and Swanston Street (walk 3) in central Melbourne.

RECOMMENDED TOURS FOR...

FOODIES

This food-obsessed city promises a gourmet experience par excellence. The best eateries are in the central city, but there are also gems at Crown Casino (walk 7), on Domain Road (walk 8) and in St Kilda (walk 11).

MODERN ARCHITECTURE

Melbourne's Victorian-era buildings are marvellous, but the city's modern architecture is perhaps even more eye-catching. Don't miss Federation Square or the cutting-edge constructions along Swanston Street (both walk 3).

ETHNIC ENCLAVES

Few cities are as ethnically diverse as Melbourne. Enjoy an espresso in Little Italy (walk 4), scoff a bagel with Balaclava's Jewish community (walk 11) or try Chinese *yum cha* in Little Bourke Street (walk 2).

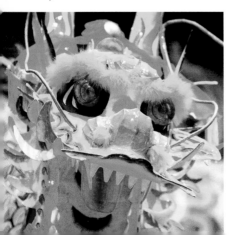

BOHEMIAN MELBOURNE

Call it bohemian, grungy or alternative, this city has art, fashion and literary subcultures like no other. To experience them, hang out in Carlton (walk 4), Fitzroy (walk 5), Flinders Lane (walk 3) or St Kilda (walk 11).

GALLERY GOERS

Melbourne's impressive art galleries include the National Gallery of Victoria in St Kilda Road (walk 8) and the Australian Centre for Contemporary Art close by (walk 10). To check out edgy commercial spaces, try Flinders Lane (walk 3) or Gertrude Street in Fitzroy (walk 5).

GARDENS

It's called the 'Garden State' for good reason. Victoria's glorious gardens include the sculpture-laden grounds at historic Werribee Park (tour 14) and the world-renowned Royal Botanic Gardens (walk 8). Closer to the city centre, the Fitzroy Gardens (walk 6) and Carlton Gardens (walk 4) are just as fine.

HISTORY DEVOTEES

See where bushranger Ned Kelly was hanged (walk 4), where the Royal Australian Navy was established (walk 12), where the colonial gentry liked to party (walk 9) and where the world's first narrative film was made (walk 2).

THE SEASIDE

If you do love to be beside the seaside, dine overlooking fashionable St Kilda Beach (walk 11), bathe at Williamstown Beach (walk 12) or set off down the Great Ocean Road (tour 14).

SPORTS FANS

Think Melbourne, think sport. This is where the first Test cricket match was played (walk 7), where the world's most famous surfing carnival is held (tour 14) and where the first event of the annual international Formula One Grand Prix circuit kicks off (walk 10).

OVERVIEW

An overview of Melbourne's geography, character and culture, plus illuminating background information on food and drink, shopping, entertainment, sporting events and history.

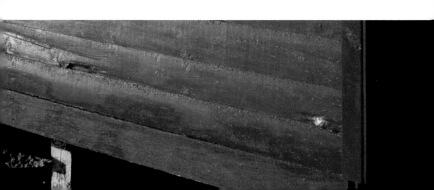

CITY INTRODUCTION

Many of the world's great cities have taken millennia to develop their vibrant, rich and many-layered cultures; Melbourne has done it over a mere two centuries, while being inclusive and egalitarian to boot.

The city has come a long way since 1835, when farmer John Batman and businessman John Pascoe Fawkner laid down their hats to call it home. It wasn't long before the fledgling settlement became a town and the town became one of the great cities of the southern hemisphere, sped on its way by the discovery of gold and an influx of people from every corner of the globe. Their optimism, ambition and hard work have made Melbourne what it is today – a city formed by dreams and characterised by diversity.

GEOGRAPHY AND LAYOUT

Melbourne is the largest city in the state of Victoria, which occupies the southeastern corner of Australia. It is arranged around the shores of Port Phillip Bay, a large inland bay separated from Bass Strait by the Bellarine Peninsula in the southwest and the Mornington Peninsula in the southeast. Roughly equidistant between the two peninsulas is the mouth of the Yarra River, where Europeans first settled and where the CBD (Central Business District) is located today.

City Layout

The inner city covers an area radiating out approximately 7km (4 miles) from the CBD and has an extremely high population density, particularly in the CBD and St Kilda. It is very easy to navigate, with the CBD on the northern banks of the Yarra having been laid out in a grid pattern by surveyor Robert Hoddle in the 1830s.

A number of inner-city suburbs can easily be accessed on foot from the CBD. Just to the north are the parks and tree-lined boulevards of Carlton, as well as the shabby-chic shopping and entertainments streets of neighbouring Fitzroy. Across the Yarra River, beyond the modern developments of Southbank and the green lungs of the Kings Domain and Royal Botanic Gardens, are the upmarket suburbs of South Melbourne and South Yarra. Other suburbs, such as seaside St Kilda, can be accessed via frequent trams, buses or trains.

Greater Melbourne

The city has one of the largest urban footprints in the world due to its ever-increasing low-density suburban sprawl (it is currently the fastest-growing city in Australia). Greater Melbourne

sprawls eastwards through the wine- and cheese-producing Yarra Valley towards the Dandenong Ranges and northwards towards the foothills of the Macedon and Great Dividing ranges. It also incorporates the area down to the start of the Mornington Peninsula at Frankston, in the city's southeast, and the satellite suburbs of Werribee and Melton in the west.

ARCHITECTURE

Marvellous Melbourne

Melbourne's foundation and early development corresponded roughly with the rule of Queen Victoria (1819–1901), and much of the inner city's architecture is Victorian in style. Locally, it is sometimes called 'Boom style' architecture, although architectural historians divide it into sub-styles such as Georgian Colonial, Gothic Revival, Renaissance Revival and French Second Empire. The National Trust of Australia (Victoria) has long fought to preserve the unique character of its Victorian streets, declaring many of them Urban Conservation Areas and lobbying the State Government for their preservation and protection. Rows of grand terrace housing adorned with cast-iron lace are scattered throughout the inner-city suburbs, often overlooking formal squares and gardens. Terraces of far more modest workers' cottages – some timber, some brick – also date from this time.

The grand public buildings from this period are quite extraordinary, and make the CBD a veritable treasure trove of 19th-century architecture. Built with gold-rush money, these buildings were often inspired by fashionable buildings in the 'Mother Country', specifically London. Collins Street (see p.28) is full of such buildings. The most significant Victorian-style building in Melbourne is the Royal Exhibition Building in Carlton (see p.50), completed in 1880 and now included on Unesco's World Heritage List.

Above from far left: the Melbourne Safe Deposit building in Queen Street is typical of the Gothic Revival style; view of the CBD from the banks of the Yarra.

Below: Federation Square, the city's showpiece plaza.

Art Deco and Modernism

Although there are Edwardian, Art Nouveau and Beaux Arts-style buildings in the city, they are relatively few in number. The next major architectural style to be adopted was Art Deco. Major city thoroughfares including Swanston Street *(see p.41)* and Bourke Street *(see p.34)* sport many buildings designed in the Jazz Moderne, Moderne or Streamline Moderne subsets of this style.

The logical design heir to Art Deco was Modernism, and this was another style embraced in Melbourne with alacrity. Orica House *(see p.57)* is the finest example in central Melbourne, but many buildings at the western end of Collins and Bourke streets are almost as impressive.

Local architects flirted with Brutalism in the 1970s and enjoyed a brief encounter or two with Postmodernism in the 1970s, but it is safe to say that Melbourne's architects and developers have remained faithful to Modernism. In fact, its pared-back, sleek and sophisticated packaging is the very quintessence of the city.

CLIMATE

Melbourne is well known for its changeable weather conditions. This is due in part to the city's flat topography, its situation on Port Phillip Bay and the presence of the Dandenong Ranges to the east, a combination that creates weather systems that often circle the bay.

The city has warm to hot summers. January and February are the hottest months, and the maximum temperature can reach a sweltering 40°C (104°F) and beyond on some days. The summer average maximum is 26°C (79°F) and the average minimum is 14°C (57°F). In winter the average maximum temperature is 14°C and the minimum 6°C (43°C), although wind chill can make it seem much cooler. The best time to visit is during autumn or spring, when temperatures are mild and skies relatively clear. However, early or long winters are not unusual.

A Labyrinth of Laneways

Every city has a visual signature. Some have a distinctive skyline, others an iconic building or a natural feature. Melbourne has none of these. Instead, the city centre is distinguished by a labyrinth of laneways where graffiti artists work, alternative bars flourish and bohemian boutiques proliferate.

These lanes started life in the 1840s and 1850s as ad hoc service routes to large commercial buildings fronting the major east–west boulevards, and were only traversed by nightsoil carts, delivery vans and rubbish collectors. Today, laneways such as Flinders Lane, Little Collins Street, Little Bourke Street and Little Lonsdale Street are among the most vibrant thoroughfares in the CBD, and the diminutive detours off them are the province of edgy street art and even edgier street cafés and bars.

For a taste of this city phenomenon, check out Oliver Lane, Hosier Lane and Degraves Street between Flinders Lane and Flinders Street; Block Place; and Caledonian Lane between Little Bourke Street and Lonsdale Street.

THE MELBURNIANS

Melbourne is one of the world's most ethnically and culturally diverse cities. Of Greater Melbourne's population of just over 4 million (the second-largest urban population in Australia after Sydney), almost a third were born overseas. The largest migrant groups come from the UK, Italy, Vietnam, China, New Zealand, Greece, India, Sri Lanka and Malaysia, although arrivals from African nations such as Sudan and Ethiopia have been growing in recent years. This heritage is reflected in the rich variety of eating options in the city.

With an average age of 36, Melbourne is a young person's city too, more so in densely populated inner-city areas such as the CBD, South Yarra and St Kilda rather than in the suburbs.

Local Customs

Australian culture generally lacks pretensions. You are more likely to be greeted with a 'G'day mate' than a stiff 'How do you do', and while friends and family may kiss cheeks in the European style, mere acquaintances wouldn't dream of doing so, relying instead on firm handshakes to greet both sexes.

Sport is huge in Melbourne, especially footy (Australian Rules, naturally), cricket, swimming, basketball, soccer, netball, golf and athletics. Some spectators are knowledgeable, bordering on the obsessive, but others are merely along for a good day out. And locals are just as likely to flock to cultural events (especially festivals), dine out or make weekly pilgrimages to the city's historic produce markets (especially the Queen Victoria).

Mealtimes generally correspond with those in Britain (lunch between noon–2pm and dinner between 7–9pm). The only difference is that in hot weather, locals tend to eat a bit later and rely heavily on the barbecue.

Many businesses (including some restaurants) close down from Christmas Day until mid-January, during which time Melburnians decamp down the coast for their annual – and sacrosanct – beach holiday.

A LIVEABLE CITY

The Mercer Quality of Living Survey and *The Economist* World's Most Liveable Cities Index regularly list Melbourne as one of the world's most liveable cities. It's easy to see why. The city's air is clean, its suburbs are green and its streets are safe. Public transport is good and the cost of living is relatively low. Melbourne's diverse population endows day-to-day life with a cultural richness, inclusivity and complexity seen in very few Western societies; it has thriving arts and sports scenes; and its focus on the enjoyable elements of life – including outdoor activities and some of the world's best food, wine and coffee – make it a truly fabulous place in which to work, live or stay.

Above from far left: kangaroos outside the Royal Exhibition Building in Carlton Gardens; Melbourne has a rocking live music scene; window cleaning, Fed Square; meeting friends outside Flinders Street Station.

Below: fanatical about sport.

FOOD AND DRINK

These days, Australia is as renowned for its cuisine as it is for its natural attractions (and that's saying a lot). Each of the capital cities has a great food scene, but Melbourne's has long been considered the king of them all.

Restaurants in Melbourne function as global culinary incubators; many young chefs train locally and then leave for further experience on foreign shores, where they end up forging stellar reputations.

The favour is returned by scores of overseas chefs who do the opposite and make their lives and careers here after training with top-notch restaurants around the world. In fact, it can sometimes seem as if there are more chefs working in Melbourne who have done multiple stints in Michelin-starred restaurants than there are locally trained equivalents. These talented imports are lured here by peerless fresh produce, exciting fusions of flavours, a devoted foodie culture and an attitude to fine dining that stresses fun rather than formality.

MELBOURNE'S CUISINE

There's no one tag for Melbourne's cuisine. You can eat everything from classic French dishes to spicy Malaysian hawker food, simple Mediterranean favourites to molecular tours de force à la Heston Blumenthal. The only thing that's uniform is the excellence and affordability of the local food and wine – indulging your tastebuds here is a supremely satisfying experience.

Fresh Produce

Fresh, locally sourced produce is used by chefs across the city, with many having a particular penchant for organic artisan ingredients. Menus are likely to specify meat producers (grass-fed and Wagyu beef from East Gippsland is favoured), the provenance of cheese (look out for offerings from Gippsland and the Yarra Valley), where salt is sourced (the pink grains from Murray River are often used) and the waters from which seafood has been sourced (Pacific oysters and Coffin Bay scallops from neighbouring South Australia are hugely popular).

International Ingredients

Imported artisan products also feature, with tapas bars using Ortiz anchovies, *jamón serrano* and *queso manchego*, and Italian restaurants eschewing local equivalents for the best Carnaroli and Vialone Nano rice, Parmigiano Reggiano cheese and Italian olive oils (although the quality of local olive oil is improving every day).

Good Food Guide
The local foodie bible is the *Good Food Guide* (http://m.gfg. theage.com.au) published by *The Age* newspaper. Each year the guide's food critics award chef hats (a star equivalent) to the best eateries in Victoria. The ultimate accolade is a three-hat rating, but a one- or two-hat rating is also impressive, ensuring both clients and the respect of the food-and-wine community.

International Cuisine

The Italian, French and Chinese (specifically Cantonese) cuisines have long pedigrees in Melbourne, but food from Spain, Lebanon, Morocco, Thailand, Malaysia, Turkey, Vietnam and Ethiopia is becoming increasingly popular, and many of the city's most exciting restaurants showcase these cuisines.

Interestingly – and perhaps this is the key to the success of Australian cuisine generally – a chef will draw on cuisines from across the globe for inspiration and when putting together a menu. A fragrant red Thai curry might sit next to a perfectly chargrilled rib-eye served with mash, and a delicate panna cotta might share the spotlight with mango-topped sticky rice. In Melbourne the brave new world of contemporary international food is as exciting as it is assured.

WHERE TO EAT

Some cuisines are strongly associated with particular streets or suburbs – Footscray and Richmond are full of Vietnamese restaurants, for instance – but this is less the case now than it has been in the past. Most suburbs have eating options in every budget category, although restaurants at the higher end of the spectrum tend to be found in central Melbourne, South Yarra and St Kilda.

High-End Restaurants

Australians are an egalitarian bunch and tend to view formal fine-dining establishments with a certain degree of suspicion. Epicures are just as likely to get excited about the menu at an edgy inner-suburban tapas bar as they are at restaurants in possession of a rare three-hat rating *(see margin, left)*, and those who dine out regularly tend to focus their attention on one- or two-hat establishments.

There are only two restaurants in town with three-hat status: Jacques Reymond in Windsor and Vue de Monde in central Melbourne. Both offer simply extraordinary dining

Above from far left: David's, a Chinese restaurant and one of the city's many ethnic eateries; fresh ingredients are paramount; Acland Street in St Kilda is lined with cake shops; a two-hat-rated restaurant.

Below: deli produce at Queen Victoria Market.

experiences. These places are expensive – set menus hover around A$150 per person – and have wonderful wine lists. You will need to book ahead for both, and Vue de Monde insists on receiving credit-card details when reserving a table; if you don't show, you will be charged for the meal regardless.

There is a slew of upscale restaurants at Crown Casino too, including Nobu, Spice Temple, Rockpool Bar & Grill and Bistro Guillaume. St Kilda has Circa at The Prince hotel, South Yarra has The Botanical and Central Melbourne has Taxi Dining Room and ezard at The Adelphi hotel. You should dress to impress at all of these, and also come with a fully charged credit card.

Mid-Range Restaurants

This is the category that Melburnians love the most. Often, the food on offer is just as impressive as that served in the high-end establishments, the differences being that the vibe will be more casual, the wine lists less encyclopaedic, the service less formal and the prices more reasonable. The vast majority offer menus heavy on Mediterranean choices, with occasional forays into Asia.

Many of these places match a stylish interior with an impressive menu, interesting wine list and professional service. Two-hat places sitting comfortably in this category include Grossi Florentino's upstairs restaurant, Donovans, Café Di Stasio and Matteo's.

Ethnic Restaurants

In times past, describing a Melbourne restaurant as 'ethnic' hinted at over-spiced dishes (usually with Indian overtones), a hippie interior and Ravi Shankar on the sound system. Not any more, though.

After a week or so here, visitors to Melbourne inevitably opine that the most exciting and enjoyable restaurants are those that combine a designer interior with a bustling ambience and specific ethnic cuisine. Supreme among these are the Spanish MoVida, pan-Asian Gingerboy, Thai Longrain, Lebanese/Persian Rumi and Turkish Gigibaba.

Yum cha (dim sum) is a weekend institution, as is a pre-dinner tapas indulgence or an antipasti-fuelled *aperitivo* in an inner-city bar/restaurant.

Also of note is the takeaway food on offer here. Streets such as Sydney Road in Brunswick are littered with places specialising in cheap and tasty falafel sandwiches and *pides* (Turkish pizza-like flatbread), and you will find rice-paper rolls and *pho* (noodle soup) in many Footscray and Richmond cafés. Whether you are after a samosa, souvlaki or sushi roll, you are bound to find a vendor somewhere.

Pubs

The phenomenon of the gastro pub hasn't really hit Melbourne. Instead, many corner pubs across the inner city have been reinvented as attitude-free

Produce Markets

Melbourne is known throughout Australia for the excellence of its fresh produce markets. The best of these are the historic Queen Victoria Market *(see p.39)* and Prahran Market *(see p.71)*, both of which are home to hundreds of specialist food stalls. There are also many farmers' markets around town, including the Slow Food Melbourne Farmers' Market (www.mfm.com.au) at the Abbotsford Convent on the fourth Saturday of every month.

drinking zones that have undergone funky fitouts and offer well-priced and imaginative bar meals. Notable examples include The Lincoln Hotel in Carlton and The Builder's Arms in Fitzroy, but there are many others where the menu is more likely to feature a spicy calamari stir-fry or fragrant chicken tagine and couscous as it is a plate of steak, eggs and chips. Those pubs with a beer garden tend to be hugely popular in summer.

DRINKS

Beer

Most Aussies like a beer or two. Brits might get a shock when they realise that lager, rather than ale, is all that's on offer, but they are usually swiftly reconciled to their fate.

You will find the local drops Carlton and VB on tap at most pubs, and bars tend to have one of the two on tap as well. Boutique alternatives such as Cooper's, Cascade, Mountain Goat and Little Creatures are often available on tap and always in bottles. Imported beers are also widely available. There are three glass sizes: a glass (200ml), pot (285ml) or pint (570ml).

Wine

Australia is one of the most highly respected New World wine-producing countries. Regions such as the Barossa, Coonawarra, Clare Valley, Margaret River, Yarra Valley and Mornington

Peninsula produce exceptionally fine vintages year after year, and locals are just as likely to order a glass of Shiraz or Sauvignon Blanc when they go out for a drink as they are a cocktail or beer. Those keen to sample Victorian wines should opt for Shiraz from the Heathcote region, Pinot Noir, Chardonnay or sparkling wine from the Yarra Valley, or Pinot Noir and Chardonnay from the Mornington Peninsula, Bellarine Peninsula and Gippsland.

James Halliday's informative Australian Wine Companion website (www.winecompanion.com.au) and *Wine Atlas of Australia* are excellent references for those wanting to learn more about local wines.

Above from far left: Mediterranean-style lunch; Aussie lager.

Below: popular tapas bar MoVida.

SHOPPING

Melburnians love nothing more than a generous dose of retail therapy. Conspicuous consumption was a hallmark of the gold-rush era, and locals have been flashing their credit cards and cash in city stores ever since.

Opening Times
Most shops are open Mon–Wed 10am–5.30pm, Thur–Fri 10am–7pm or 9pm and Sat 10am–5pm. Many shops in central Melbourne also open on Sunday from 11am or noon–4pm.

The local shopping scene is quite distinctive, being unusually heavy on quirky boutiques, designer outlets and gourmet food stores. Sure, there are malls and chain stores, but these tend to be on the city's outer fringe, rarely frequented by visitors or locals seeking unique merchandise. The latter have turned shopping into an art form – they know where to find the most attractive designer jewellery, the hippest homewares and the edgiest ensembles. One day they may be buying Thai silk to use for making cushions, the next they will be visiting their local op (thrift) shop to see what pre-loved gems await. Such shopaholics are particularly in evidence during March's L'Oréal Melbourne Fashion Festival (www.lmff.com.au).

Below: funky footwear in Prahran; Buddha kitsch in Chinatown.

SHOPPING AREAS

Central Melbourne
If you can't find it in the city, it probably doesn't exist. Central Melbourne is home to the Myer and David Jones department stores, the fashionable GPO and QV shopping centres, global luxury brands such as Chanel and Gucci, and flagship stores for the major book retailers.

Far more interesting are the small designer boutiques clustered in the city's laneways, streets and arcades. For Australian-designed jewellery, e.g.etal in Flinders Lane and Little Collins Street is hard to beat; for a wide-brimmed Akubra hat, City Hatters in Flinders Street Station is the place to go. Fashionable accessories from Australia and overseas tempt anyone who ventures into Christine, and stylish handmade items crowd the shelves at Counter, the retail arm of Craft Victoria – both are located on Flinders Lane. Edgy and affordable outfits can be admired at Genki in Swanston Street's Cathedral Arcade, and at Alice Euphemia in the same arcade.

Gertrude and Brunswick Streets
Accessories, toiletries and alternative and vintage fashion are strongly represented on these streets in Fitzroy *(see pp.54–6)*. Australia's famous Crumpler brand has its flagship bag store on Gertrude Street, and its neighbours include local brands Aesop, known for its natural skin, hair and body products, and Vixen, famous for body-hugging clothing made using distinctive screen-printed fabrics. Further west is the

unassuming Cottage Industry, a fashion and accessory store that balances charm, style and affordability with great success.

Brunswick Street has boutiques galore, including the exquisite Kleins Perfumery and quirky Koko jewellery store. Other favourites include Douglas and Hope for fashion and homewares, and T2 for tea and tea-making accessories. Simon Johnson, in nearby St David Street, is the place to go for Australian and imported gourmet foods.

Chapel Street

Come to Chapel Street in Prahran *(see pp. 70–1)* for local fashion labels Bettina Liano, Alannah Hill, Collette Dinnigan and Scanlan & Theodore. Travel southwards to find the funky Chapel Street Bazaar, home to vintage furniture and bric-a-brac. Foodies flock to The Essential Ingredient, in Prahran Market on Commercial Road, which stocks a huge range of gourmet foods and homewares.

High Street and Malvern Road

This is where you will find antiques and designer homewares. These chichi strips – running parallel through Prahran, Armadale and Malvern – are where ladies lunch and give their husbands' salaries regular workovers. Big names include Graham Geddes Antiques and Antique Decor in High Street and John D. Dunn Antiques in Malvern Road. Fashion boutiques worth checking out include Husk in Malvern Road.

This is also where the art and antiques auction houses are located. Bonhams & Goodman is on Malvern Road in Prahran, Leonard Joel is on Malvern Road in South Yarra, Philips Auctions is on Glenferrie Road in Malvern and Sotheby's is on High Street in Armadale.

Coventry Street

Homewares are strongly represented on the stretch of Coventry Street between Clarendon and Cecil streets in South Melbourne *(see p. 75)*. Look out for Nest, Macphees for the Wine Enthusiast, Made in Japan and R. G. Madden.

Above from far left: boomerangs handcrafted by Aboriginal Australians; boutique shops and cafés line a laneway.

Sales
The major annual sales are after Christmas (from Boxing Day onwards) and at Easter, although bargains can usually be had at the end of each season.

Bookshop Bonanza

Melbourne is well known for its impressive independent bookshops. Chief among these are the five stores in the Readings group, located in Carlton, St Kilda, Hawthorn, Port Melbourne, Malvern and the State Library of Victoria. The flagship Carlton store is one of the city's main literary salons, hosting book launches and literary events galore.

Other stores well worth a browse include Reader's Feast on the corner of Swanston and Bourke streets in the CBD, The Avenue Bookstore in Albert Park, The Paperback Bookshop and Hill of Content stores at the top end of Bourke Street in the CBD, and the Brunswick Street Bookstore in Fitzroy.

Collectors of antiquarian books gravitate towards Kay Craddock in Collins Street, gay and lesbian readers adore Hares & Hyenas in Fitzroy and poetry lovers linger among the shelves at Collected Works in Swanston Street's Nicholas Building.

A good chain bookshop is Dymocks at 234 Collins Street, while the Foreign Language Bookstore at 259 Collins Street stocks books in over 100 different languages.

ENTERTAINMENT

Often described as Australia's cultural capital, Melbourne takes its artistic entertainments seriously. It is rare to encounter a night when a cutting-edge performance of one type or another isn't being staged around town.

Listings

The best listings for Melbourne's lively performing arts scene can be found in the *Entertainment Guide* (EG) published every Friday in *The Age* newspaper.

For a selection of nightlife listings, *see pp.122–3.*

Cut-Price Tickets

For discounted tickets to theatre, comedy, opera, dance and live music perfomances, visit the Half-tix box office by the Town Hall on Swanston Street *(see p.44).* Tickets are usually sold on the day of the performance and only cash payments are accepted.

The opening-night scene dominates the city's social calendar, and arts companies receive a healthy slice of the corporate philanthropic pie. A decent allocation of local-, state- and federal-government money is also dedicated to the performing arts. Many directors have done their artistic apprenticeships here and gone on to make strong impressions overseas, with recent examples being Jonathan Mills (current Director of the Edinburgh International Festival) and Barrie Kosky (newly appointed Chief Director at the Komische Oper in Berlin). Hundreds of local performers have international reputations and careers, but choose to retain Melbourne as their home base, attracted by the diversity of work on offer, appreciative audiences and excellent venues.

THEATRE

Melbourne has a vibrant theatre scene. The major professional company is the Melbourne Theatre Company (www. mtc.com.au), its productions appearing in two venues – the MTC Theatre at Southbank and the Arts Centre at St Kilda Road. It is one of the English-speaking world's largest theatre companies, staging up to 12 plays a season. The state's second company is the Malthouse Theatre (www.malt housetheatre.com.au) on Sturt Street in Southbank.

Theatrical events including musicals are staged at the Arts Centre *(see p.63),* Her Majesty's Theatre (www.hmt.com. au) and the Princess, Regent and Comedy theatres (www.marrinerthe atres.com.au) in the central city. More adventurous work can be found at fortyfivedownstairs (www.fortyfive downstairs.com) in Flinders Lane, Red Stitch Actors' Theatre (www. redstitch.net) in East St Kilda, La Mama (www.lamama.com.au) in Carlton and Theatreworks (www.theatre works.org.au) in St Kilda.

DANCE

The national ballet company, the Australian Ballet (www.australianballet. com.au), is based here. It performs at the Arts Centre's State Theatre. The current artistic director, David Mc-Allister, is a former principal artist with the company; his predecessor was Ross Stretton who left the company to take up the role of artistic director of

the Royal Ballet, Covent Garden.

Chunky Move (www.chunkymove.com) is known internationally for its programme of genre-defying dance performance. It usually performs at the Malthouse Theatre.

Dancehouse (www.dancehouse.com.au) is an alternative dance venue in North Carlton.

MUSIC

Classical

The Melbourne Symphony Orchestra (www.mso.com.au) is Australia's oldest orchestra and has an excellent reputation. It performs at a variety of locations, including the Melbourne Town Hall *(see p.44)* and the Arts Centre. In summer (usually February) it performs free concerts at the Sidney Myer Music Bowl *(see p.68)*. Other classical concerts are staged at the Melbourne Recital Centre (www.melbournerecital.com.au) on Southbank Boulevard.

Although based in Sydney, Opera Australia (www.opera-australia.org.au) has Melbourne seasons at the Arts Centre's State Theatre in April–June and October–December.

Jazz

The main venue in town is Bennetts Lane (www.bennettslane.com).

The Australian Art Orchestra (www.aao.com.au) is the country's premier contemporary music ensemble.

Rock and Pop

Melbourne's rock scene is based in pub venues. To check who's playing in town, tune into radio stations 3RRR (102.7 FM), 3MMM (105.1 FM) and 3PBS (106.7 FM) or grab a copy of the EG *(see margin, left)*. The Esplanade Hotel (The Espy; www.espy.com.au) and Prince Bandroom *(see p.123)* in St Kilda host local, interstate and international acts, as do the Corner Hotel (www.cornerhotel.com) in Richmond, The Tote (www.thetotehotel.com) in Collingwood, the Northcote Social Club (www.northcotesocialclub.com) and the East Brunswick Club (www.eastbrunswickclub.com).

FILM

Melbourne has a strong arthouse cinema scene, with popular venues including Cinema Nova (www.cinemanova.com.au) in Carlton, Kino Cinemas (www.palacecinemas.com.au) in the city centre, and the Como in South Yarra (www.palacecinemas.com.au). The high-profile Melbourne International Film Festival (www.melbournefilmfestival.com.au) is held in July/August each year at venues across central Melbourne.

Mainstream multiplexes are located across the city and suburbs, including at Melbourne Central on the corner of La Trobe and Swanston streets, and Crown Casino at Southbank.

Above from far left: live music at the Ding Dong Lounge; posters in Las Chicas café in St Kilda; the Malthouse theatre.

Arts Festivals
Melbourne's flagship cultural event, the Melbourne International Arts Festival (www.melbourne festival.com.au), is held in October each year. It features a world-class line-up of theatre, music, dance and visual arts. Other festivals include the Melbourne International Comedy Festival (www.comedy festival.com.au) in April, the Melbourne International Jazz Festival (www.melbournejazz.com) usually April/May, and the Melbourne Fringe Festival (www.melbournefringe.com.au) usually August.

SPORTING EVENTS

Melburnians may enjoy cultural pursuits, but they enjoy spectator sport much, much more. Woe betide those who publicly profess to have no interest in tennis, cricket and football – they are treated with a mixture of disbelief and disdain by the sports-mad majority.

Moonah Classic
The PGA Australian Open is held in Sydney, but Melbourne has its own major golf tournament, the AUD$850,000 Moonah Classic (www.moonahlinks. com.au), held on the Mornington Peninsula. This event is sanctioned by the US Nationwide Tour as part of its 'Down Under Swing'.

Beach Events
Victoria's famous Great Ocean Road hosts two high-profile sporting events each year – The Rip Curl Pro Surf at Easter and the Lorne Pier to Pub swim in January. For more details, *see p.94 and p.95.*

Images of bronzed Aussie athletes often adorn tourist brochures, but true Aussie sports aficionados don't usually resemble this stereotype. In fact, they are far more likely to be slightly overweight chaps sitting in the stands and watching a sporting match while scoffing a meat pie and downing a beer. That said, there's something enormously endearing about the general obsession with spectator sport here, and locals have truly got it down to an art form. They know that the Melbourne Cricket Ground's Southern Stand is where they should be on Boxing Day, that they should take a foldout chair when queuing for tickets to the Australian Football League's finals series and that sunblock and bottled water are essential when spectating in summer. If attending a major sporting event while in town, you are bound to be bowled over by the infectious enthusiasm, fierce partisanship and general bonhomie evident in the crowd.

AFL SEASON

The AFL (Australian Football League) season starts in March each year and culminates in the finals series in September. Melbourne goes footy crazy during the finals – club colours are seen everywhere, pubs show televised matches on big screens, finals barbecues are popular and there's even a street parade in central Melbourne on the Friday before the Grand Final. The Grand Final itself is played at the MCG *(see p.61)* on the last Saturday of the month before a crowd of 100,000. Unfortunately, tickets for all finals matches are extremely hard to come by; for more information see www. afl.com.au/tickets.

AUSTRALIAN FORMULA ONE GRAND PRIX

Locals are divided when it comes to this event – fans are loud in their support and opponents are even louder in voicing their displeasure. Held in the usually tranquil surrounds of Albert Park Lake *(see p.77)* in March each year, the four-day Australian Formula One Grand Prix (www.grandprix. com.au) certainly causes a buzz around town, particularly on Lygon Street in Carlton, which is home to a huge concentration of Ferrari fans.

SPRING RACING CARNIVAL

On the first Tuesday in November, tens of thousands of Melburnians don their smartest outfit (including a hat), grab a form guide from the newspaper and make their way to Flemington Race-course (northwest of the city centre) to one of the world's great horse races, the Melbourne Cup (www.melbournecup. com). The glitterati spend the day in lavish corporate marquees in the car park, but most punters stake out a patch of lawn or grandstand seat and settle in to enjoy peerless people-watching, great horseracing and more than a few glasses of bubbly.

Other popular Spring Carnival events are Oaks Day and Derby Day at Flemington (www.vrc.net.au), the Caulfield Cup at Caulfield Racecourse (www.melbourneracingclub.net.au) and the Cox Plate at Moonee Valley Racecourse (www.mvrc.net.au).

TENNIS

The Australian Open (www.australianopen.com) is one of the most popular events in the sporting calendar. The Grand Slam tournament for the Asia/Pacific region is held in the second half of January each year at Melbourne Park *(see p.62)* on the Yarra. The world's best slog it out in often sweltering conditions (40°C/104°F is not unusual) and the crowd is vociferous in its support of local contenders and visiting favourites.

TEST CRICKET

When locals think of summer, two things come to mind: the beach and cricket (sometimes the two are conflated in the popular pastime of beach cricket). The international season kicks off with the famous Boxing Day Test at the MCG and continues through January and into February. For more information and to buy tickets, go to the Cricket Australia website (www.cricket.com.au).

Above from far left: Aussie Rules footy; Melburnians are sport mad.

Below: at the Australian Open.

HISTORY: KEY DATES

In 1835 John Batman stood on the banks of the Yarra and noted, 'This will be the place for a village.' Two decades later, a gold rush caused the settlement to boom and become the 'Marvellous Melbourne' that it has been ever since.

EUROPEAN ARRIVALS

1802   The crew of the *Lady Nelson* are the first white men to enter the Port Phillip Bay area.

1834   Pastoralists (livestock farmers) from Van Diemen's Land establish Victoria's first long-term settlement at Portland on Bass Strait.

1835   Farmer John Batman makes a treaty with the Wurundjeri for 240,000ha (592,800 acres) of land on Port Phillip's shores, giving them blankets and trinkets in payment; Batman and businessman John Pascoe Fawkner then found a white settlement on the banks of the Yarra River.

1837   The settlement is named in honour of British prime minister Lord Melbourne; surveyor Robert Hoddle lays out central Melbourne's grid system; the first inner-city land sale.

1842   The municipality of Melbourne is created.

1845   The Princes Bridge is constructed, linking the north and south banks of the Yarra River.

1847   Queen Victoria declares Melbourne a city.

Original Owners
Port Phillip Bay and the Yarra Valley are the traditional homes of three of the five Kulin Nations: the Wathaurong, Woi-wurrung (Wurundjeri) and Boonerwrung (Bunurong). These indigenous Australians lived here for 40,000 years before white settlers arrived and took their land in 1835.

GOLD RUSH

1851   Melbourne is separated from New South Wales; gold is discovered in central Victoria, triggering a gold rush.

1852   75,000 gold-seekers arrive in the colony.

1853   The University of Melbourne is established.

1854   A railway between Port Melbourne and the central city is opened; the State Library of Victoria is founded.

1857   The train line between the central city and St Kilda begins operation.

1858   The first games of Aussie Rules Football are played.

1861   The Melbourne Cup is held for the first time – won by the horse Archer.

1877   The first Test cricket match is played at the MCG.

| 1880 | Notorious bushranger Ned Kelly is captured in Glenrowan and hanged in Melbourne; the International Exhibition is held in the newly built Royal Exhibition Building. |
| 1885 | English journalist George Augustus Sala describes the city as 'Marvellous Melbourne'; the first cable-tram line opens. |

20TH CENTURY

1901	The federation of the six colonies becomes the Commonwealth of Australia; Melbourne is made the temporary parliamentary capital.
1906	The Melbourne Symphony Orchestra is formed.
1911	The city's most famous department store, the Myer Emporium, opens.
1927	Federal parliament moves to the new national capital, Canberra.
1933	Melbourne's population passes 1 million mark.
1942	Melbourne becomes the Allied headquarters for the Southwest Pacific in World War II.
1945	Australia embarks on an immigration programme; Melbourne attracts migrants from Greece, Italy and Malta.
1956	The Olympic Games are held in Melbourne.
1961	Melbourne's population passes 2 million.
1967	The first female city councillor is elected.
1973	The 'White Australia' policy is overturned and Melbourne sees a huge increase in immigrants from Southeast Asia.
1982	City subway loop opens.
1990	Southbank Promenade is completed, opening the city to the southern banks of the Yarra.
1996	Development of the Docklands begins.

21ST CENTURY

2002	Federation Square opens.
2006	Melbourne hosts Commonwealth Games.
2008	Prime Minister Kevin Rudd officially apologises to Aboriginal Australians of the 'Stolen Generations'.
2009	Bushfires sweep through many parts of Victoria, including the Yarra Valley; deaths total nearly 200.
2010	Julia Gillard, a Welsh-born Australian, becomes the first female prime minister of Australia.

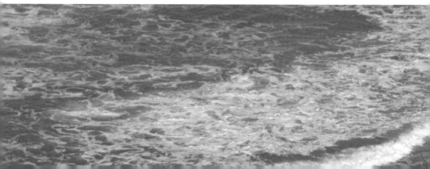

WALKS AND TOURS

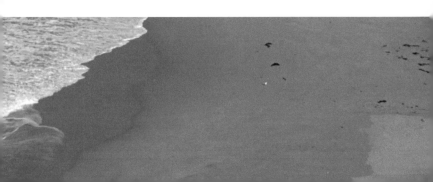

COLLINS STREET

Aficionados of architecture will be in seventh heaven as they stroll the length of this famous city street. An open museum of significant 19th- and 20th-century buildings, including opulent Block Arcade and the soaring Rialto Towers, it is also known for its plane trees and upmarket shops.

DISTANCE 2km (1¼ miles)

TIME Six hours

START Southern Cross Railway Station

END City Museum

POINTS TO NOTE

Combine this route with walks 2 and 3 for a rewarding two-day exploration of central Melbourne.

Named after Lieutenant-Governor David Collins, who led the unsuccessful attempt to settle at Sorrento (south of Melbourne) in 1803, Collins Street has always been the place where the city's establishment chooses to conduct its business. Melbourne's stock exchange has been located here since its founda-

tion in 1884, and banks and insurance agents started trading from Collins Street premises as early as 1838. Most of these early businessmen and bankers were based west of Swanston Street, with the blocks to the east hosting a diverse mix of artists' studios, medical consulting rooms, upmarket boutiques, churches and gentlemen's clubs. Today, Collins Street is recognised as the grande dame of Melbourne's boulevards, and the majority of its buildings are protected by heritage legislation.

SOUTHERN CROSS RAILWAY STATION

Begin in front of **Southern Cross Railway Station ❶**, designed by British architect Nicholas Grimshaw in asso-

ciation with local firm Daryl Jackson. Completed in 2006, it has won a swag of national and international architectural awards. With its massive scale, airy interior and sensuously undulating roof, the building has endowed the western gateway to the city centre with the visual gravitas it has long deserved. The unadorned and uninspired bus exchange and retail mall to the rear and north of Grimshaw's structure is an unfortunate tacked-on addition. From the station, walk east into Collins Street.

SPENCER STREET
TO WILLIAM STREET

Lovers of Modernist architecture from the early 20th century will appreciate the **Former McPherson's Hardware Showrooms ❷** at nos 546–566 Collins Street. The curves of this 1935 building may be more subtle than those of Southern Cross Station, but they pack quite a visual punch, especially when married with the elongated horizontal form of the building, glossy black tiles and a profusion of glass.

Rialto Precinct

From the King Street corner, you will see the towering glass **Rialto Towers ❸** on your right. Completed in 1986, the towers were for many years the tallest structure in Australia, famous for their sunset-reflecting mirrored glass. Now trumped by Eureka Tower *(see p.64)*, they are still arguably the city's best-recognised landmarks. The renowned three-hat restaurant **Vue de Monde** *(see p.118)* has taken over the former observation deck on the 55th floor of the Rialto Towers after relocating from Little Collins Street.

Cowering at the towers' base are the charming 1891 **Rialto** and **Winfield buildings** at nos 487–503, once home to offices, warehouse space and the Melbourne Wool Exchange, but now occupied by the refurbished Intercontinental Melbourne Hotel (previously the Rialto Hotel). At the Towers' forecourt, adjacent to the hotel is **Merchant** *(see p.117)*, another restaurant by famous chef Guy Grossi. East of the Winfield Building are the façades of the **New Zealand Insurance Building**, Record

Above from far left: atrium at 161 On Collins, one of the street's many temples to commerce; Rialto Towers; mosaic evoking Collins Street's history.

Below: the Rialto Building viewed from Flinders Lane; statue of John Batman on Collins Street.

Above from left: names of immigrants to Australia; buildings on Bank Place.

Chambers and **Olderfleet** at nos 471–485. The Venetian Gothic-style Insurance Building dates from 1888 and is sited next to the French Renaissance-style Records Chamber, which predates it by one year. Best of all, though, is the over-the-top Gothic Revival façade of the Olderfleet, designed by William Pitt (who also designed the Rialto Building) in 1889. Sadly, most of the fabric of these buildings was lost in 1985, replaced by a glass office block.

WILLIAM STREET TO QUEEN STREET

Below: Immigration Museum, on Flinders Street.

Past William Street you enter the city's banking and financial precinct, presided over by muscular office towers, such as

the **Royal Insurance Building ❹** at nos 430–444. Dating from 1965, this is the first in a series of exceptionally fine Modernist office buildings designed by local architectural firm Yuncken Freeman. Also of note in this block are the imposing Renaissance Revival bulk of the **Bank of Australasia** on the northwestern corner of Queen Street and the **National Mutual Building** (aka Goode House) on the southwestern corner. The latter, a Gothic Revival office block completed in 1893, is often described as one of the city's first skyscrapers.

If you are in need of breakfast, coffee or lunch, veer left into Bank Place and make your way to **Syracuse**, see ⑪①, at no. 23, or carry on and turn right into Little Collins Street to reach **Café Vue**, see ⑪②.

Immigration Museum Detour
Back on Collins Street, if you detour south into Market Street and walk two blocks downhill, you will reach one of Melbourne's major 19th-century public buildings, the **Customs House ❺**. This handsome, classically proportioned building was constructed in two stages between 1856 and 1876 on a site near the city's port. It now houses the **Immigration Museum** (400 Flinders Street; tel: 13 11 02; www.museum victoria.com.au/immigrationmuseum; daily 10am–5pm; charge for adults, children free), which mounts a changing exhibition programme that explores the often sobering but always

fascinating stories of the many migrants who have settled in Victoria.

QUEEN STREET TO ELIZABETH STREET

The jewel in the crown of the banking district, which extends into this next block, is the **ANZ Gothic Bank** ❻ (Mon–Fri 9.30am–4pm) on the north-eastern corner of Queen Street. Built between 1883–7, its exterior sports Gothic porches and delicate stone carvings, while the exquisite banking chamber known as the Cathedral Room features beautiful iron columns and sculptural capitals. There are information points inside the building that facilitate self-guided tours through the Cathedral Room and **ANZ Banking Museum** (Mon–Fri 10am–3pm; free).

Near the northwestern corner of Elizabeth Street is the city's most famous gentlemen's outfitter, **Henry Bucks** (www.henrybucks.com.au), which has traded in the city since 1890.

THE BLOCK

Situated between Elizabeth and Swanston streets, 'The Block' is as prestigious an address today as it was in its late 19th-century heyday. Then, colonial banks lined the southern side of Collins Street, and fashionable shops could be found on the northern side. In the late 19th century and early 20th century, Melburnians donned their finest outfits to 'Do the Block' on Saturday afternoons. The pivot of their promenade was the opulent **Block Arcade** ❼ at no. 282, built between 1891–3. The ornate Victorian façade of this building is impressive, but the wow factor kicks in upon viewing the opulent interior, with its ornate shopfronts, glass skylights, mosaic-tiled floor and octangular core. Inside is a Melbourne institution, the **Hopetoun Tearooms**, see ⑪③, which has been serving its famous pinwheel sandwiches and 'lamingtons' (sponge-cake squares covered with chocolate and coconut and sometimes filled with cream) for over a century. Behind the

Prophetic Panels

The three panels that grace the Newspaper House façade are by Napier Waller. They depict figures and objects representing modern advances in communication and transport. The text – 'I'll put a girdle around about the earth' – is amazingly prescient considering it dates from 1932, long before global media empires such as News Corporation achieved that very same thing.

Food and Drink

① SYRACUSE
23 Bank Place; tel: 9670 1777; www.syracuserestaurant. com.au; Mon–Fri 7.30am–late, Sat 6pm–late; $$
Occupying a 19th-century bank building, Syracuse has atmosphere and style in spades. The antiques-laden dining room, with its columns and high ceilings, is gorgeous, while the Mediterranean menu tempts all tastebuds.

② CAFÉ VUE
430 Little Collins Street; tel: 9691 3899; www.vuedemonde. com.au/cafe-vue; Mon–Fri 7am–4pm; $
Shannon Bennett's Vue de Monde is regularly voted Victoria's best restaurant. This café shares the same owner and adherence to excellence, but is cheaper, easier to get into and considerably less pretentious. Its pastries and croque monsieurs are justly famous.

③ HOPETOUN TEAROOMS
Shops 1 and 2, Block Arcade; tel: 9650 2777; www.hope tountearooms.com.au; Mon–Sat 8am–5pm, Sun 9am–5pm; $
Once run by the Victorian Ladies' Work Association, this tearoom has been a genteel choice for morning or afternoon tea since first opening its doors over a century ago.

Bohemian Memories

At the end of the 19th century many artists' studios were located at the eastern end of Collins Street, notably in Grosvenor Chambers at no. 9. Painters such as Tom Roberts, Frederick McCubbin, Charles Conder and Arthur Streeton perfected their famous brand of antipodean Impressionism in these studios and the street became known for its cultural life. Sadly, most of Grosvenor Chambers was demolished in the early 1980s to accommodate a Postmodernist office tower.

Below: Regent Theatre at night.

arcade, accessed through its northern rear entrance, is **Block Place**, a narrow laneway full of hip cafés and boutiques.

On the southern side of Collins Street, close to Swanston Street, look out for the gorgeous gilt and glass mosaic on the façade of **Newspaper House** ❽ at no. 247–249, once the headquarters of Melbourne's major evening newspaper *(see margin, p.31)*.

SWANSTON STREET TO RUSSELL STREET

The stretch from Swanston Street to Russell Street follows a relatively steep incline, and is notable for its concentration of churches and theatres.

Melbourne Athenaeum

Next door to the **Melbourne Town Hall** *(see p.44)* is the **Melbourne Athenaeum** ❾. In the 19th century

many municipalities in Victoria established Mechanics Institutes aimed at providing blue-collar workers ('mechanics') with self-improvement tools such as libraries. An institute at 184–192 Collins Street was the first of these to open (in 1839) and its original modest building was replaced by this Renaissance Revival structure in 1886. The **subscription library** (tel: 9650 3100; www.melbourneathenaeum.org. au; Mon–Tue, Thur–Fri 9.30am–5pm, Wed 11am–7pm, Sat 9.30am–1pm) on the mezzanine level still operates.

Across the road from the Athenaeum is the **Regent Theatre** (www. marrinertheatres.com.au), a grand picture palace built in 1928 that now functions as a live theatre. To the right are the **Collins Street Baptist Church** and **Scots Church**.

THE PARIS END

The stretch between Russell and Spring streets became known as the 'Paris End' of Collins Street after the Oriental Hotel at no. 17 (since demolished) opened Melbourne's first sidewalk café in the 1950s. These were the days when glamorous society ladies flocked to **Le Louvre** at nos 72–74, a glamorous boutique that occupies a small townhouse dating from 1855. While they were being fitted with a fetching frock or two, their spouses sealed business deals over cigars at the **Melbourne Club** ❿, at nos 36–50, a

gentlemen's club established way back in 1838 and in this building since 1858.

Georgian Revival Townhouses

There are many gracious Georgian Revival buildings along this strip, a number of which started life as private residences for medical practitioners, bankers, solicitors or dentists. Then, as now, a Collins Street address signified professional respectability and success.

The buildings at the top end of the street are particularly handsome – look out for **Portland House**, a townhouse and doctor's surgery dating from 1872, and **Alcaston House**, the only early multi-storey apartment building remaining in the central city. It dates from 1929–30 and is still a blue-chip residential address. On the southern side of the street, at no. 9, is the façade of **Grosvenor Chambers**, once the heart of bohemian Melbourne *(see margin, left)*.

There is a veritable banquet of restaurants to choose from in this area, the best of which are **Comme Kitchen**, see ⑭④, and **The Press Club**, see ⑭⑤.

CITY MUSEUM

At the top end of Collins Street is the **Old Treasury Building** ⑪, considered by many experts to be Australia's finest 19th-century public building. Designed in 1857 by 19-year-old John James Clark from the Public Works Department, it was completed in 1862. Today, the building on 20–70 Spring Street (tel: 9651 2233; www. oldtreasurybuilding.org.au; Sun–Fri 10am–4pm; charge) houses the **City Museum**. Here you can see several exhibitions about the city's history, architecture, art and culture. Attractions include the multimedia display 'Built on Gold' in the building's basement gold vaults.

A Refreshing End

For a drink at the end of your walk, try **Bar Lourinhã**, see ⑭⑥, which is a mere castanet click away in Little Collins Street.

Food and Drink 🍴

④ COMME KITCHEN
7 Alfred Place; tel: 9631 4000; www.comme.com.au; Mon–Fri 7am–late, Sat 5pm–late; $$
If your Blahnik-shod feet need a rest before making their way to the nearby Hermès and Ferragamo shops, this mega-stylish restaurant and wine bar is the perfect pitstop. The designer decor complements an excellent Iberian-inclined menu, and the wine list is one of the best in town.

⑤ THE PRESS CLUB
72 Flinders Street; tel: 9677 9677; www.thepressclub.com.au; Mon–Sat noon–3pm, Sun 11.30am–3pm, daily 6–10pm; $$$
In the former newspaper offices of the *Herald & Weekly Times* (hence the name), this sleek restaurant-bar is run by George Colombaris, one of Melbourne's most talented chef/restaurateurs. The menu is modern Greek.

⑥ BAR LOURINHÃ
37 Little Collins Street; tel: 9663 7890; www.barlourinha. com.au; Mon–Thur noon–11pm, Fri noon–1am, Sat 4pm–1am; $$
This sexy bar-restaurant is a perfect spot for pre-dinner or late-night cocktails, fortified wines and a range of creative share-style tapas.

BOURKE STREET

Bourke Street has a long pedigree as Melbourne's premier shopping and entertainment strip. Recent years have seen it move resolutely downmarket, but a number of historically and architecturally important buildings survive, including Parliament House and the Royal Arcade.

DISTANCE 1km (⅔ mile)
TIME A half day
START Parliament House
END GPO
POINTS TO NOTE
The stretch between Swanston and Elizabeth streets is closed to cars but is still open to trams, so watch where you walk.

Crowned by the imposing edifice of Parliament House, Bourke Street can safely be described as Melbourne's main street. In the 1850s it was a crowded and rough entertainment precinct full of sly grog shops, billiard rooms, cigar divans, bowling alleys and sideshows. By the 1870s it had transformed itself into a fashionable boulevard full of shops and theatres, and was often compared with London's Oxford Street.

Below: façade at Parliament House.

Generations of Melburnians have used the description 'Busier than Bourke Street on a Saturday Night', and while the street is no longer a thriving entertainment strip, it still packs a punch when it comes to retail therapy. The city's two big department stores are located here, as are the boutique shopping complex GPO and the historic Royal Arcade.

PARLIAMENT HOUSE

Christened as the home of the Parliament of Victoria in 1856, **Parliament House ❶** (corner Spring and Bourke streets; tel: 9651 8911; www.parliament. vic.gov.au; tours at 9.30am, 10.30am, 11.30am, 1.30pm, 2.30pm, and 3.45pm when parliament is not sitting; free) also hosted the newly established Federal Parliament from 1901, only surrendering the role when legislators and the machinery of government moved to the purpose-built national capital of Canberra in 1927.

Constructed in stages, its principal spaces are the ornately decorated Leg-islative Council and Legislative Assembly Chambers (1856), Library (1860), Vestibule and Queen's Hall (1878–9), and Refreshment Rooms (1929). The classical façade and colonnade date from 1888 and the sweeping steps are a favoured location for everything from wedding party photography to political demonstrations.

Gardens

There are a number of formal gardens in the area surrounding Parliament House; these include the triangle-shaped **Parliament Gardens ❷**, the members-only Parliament House Garden and the **Gordon Reserve ❸** on the corner of Macarthur Street. This picturesque reserve is home to statues of Gordon of Khartoum and the 19th-century Australian bush poet Adam Lindsay Gordon (born 1833), who took his own life in 1870 due to money troubles. The graceful fountain in the centre of the reserve was sculpted in bluestone by William Stanford while he was incarcerated in prison in the 1860s *(see margin, right)*.

Freedom Fountain
William Stanford (1837–80) was sentenced to 22 years' imprisonment for highway robbery and horse stealing in 1860. A trained stonemason, he developed a talent for sculpture in prison. The fountain he created for Gordon Reserve was so highly regarded by the public that it led to a movement to commute his sentence. He was freed in 1870.

Above from left:
Princess Theatre;
Pellegrini's is the place
for an espresso.

Below: luxury lodgings at Hotel Windsor.

SPRING STREET TO EXHIBITION STREET

Facing the Parliament House façade are two of the city's best-loved buildings: the Princess Theatre and Hotel Windsor. Both date from Marvellous Melbourne's heyday.

Princess Theatre

The pretty-as-a-picture **Princess Theatre ❹** was designed in the French Second Empire style, and opened in 1886 with the Australian première of Gilbert & Sullivan's *The Mikado*. Notable architectural features include the mansard towers topped with cast-iron crowns and the leadlight-adorned winter garden on the first floor. Theatre lore insists that there is a resident ghost *(see margin, right)*.

Two of Melbourne's best café-wine bars sit comfortably in the Princess Theatre's shadow: the **City Wine Shop**, see ⑪①, and **The European**, see ⑪②. You will have to compete with groups of ministerial advisers from Parliament House if you decide to claim one of the outdoor tables to enjoy breakfast or a coffee. Later in the afternoon, **Melbourne Supper Club** and its **Siglo** terrace bar above The European are wonderful spots for a drink *(see p.122)*.

Hotel Windsor

The local equivalent of Singapore's Raffles or London's Savoy, the **Hotel Windsor ❺** at 111 Spring Street is one of the city's major landmarks *(see p.111)*. Opened as The Grand Coffee Palace in 1888, its owners soon gave up hope of temperance being profitable and relaunched it as the licensed Grand Hotel in 1897. The hotel's proximity to Parliament House meant that it was often treated as an extension of the parliamentary building – the federal constitution was drafted here in 1889 and it was the Melbourne residence of former prime minister Robert Menzies

(1894–1978). Renamed The Windsor in the 1920s, its north corner wing was added between 1957–63. The entire building is slated for future renovation, beginning in 2013.

Bourke Hill's Cafés

The top end of Bourke Street has long been home to a clutch of popular Italian cafés and restaurants. Many have closed in recent times, but two much-loved examples survive. **Pellegrini's** ❻, an espresso bar dating from 1955 and located at no. 66, has hardly changed in the intervening decades. It was one of the first cafés in Melbourne to possess an Italian espresso machine.

A wine bar was established at neighbouring 78–84 Bourke Street as early as 1900, but the restaurant-bar-café now known as **Grossi Florentino** ❼ dates from 1928, when the building was acquired by the Massoni family and converted into an Italian restaurant named Café Florentino. Beloved by Melbourne's establishment, the Florentino has always been split into three eating areas: a posh upstairs restaurant decorated with 16 murals depicting Renaissance Italy, a downstairs bistro and an atmospheric wine bar-café known as the **Cellar Bar**, see ⑬③.

Salvation Army Temple

Opposite Florentino, at nos 65–71, is the **Salvation Army Temple** ❽, housed in a building originally erected by the Young Men's Christian Association and acquired by the Salvation Army in 1894. Inside are a handsome auditorium with a kauri pine-vaulted ceiling and an attic studio that was the headquarters of the Salvation Army's Limelight Department. This small outfit designed and produced coloured lantern slides and photographs in the last decade of the 19th century. It was famous for creating the 1900 presentation *Soldiers of the Cross*, which

Theatrical Spirit
Performers and front-of-house staff swear that the Princess Theatre has a resident ghost, the spirit of a performer called Federici (real name Frederick Baker), a baritone who died here at the end of a performance of Gounod's *Faust* in March 1888.

Food and Drink

① CITY WINE SHOP
159 Spring Street; tel: 9654 6657; www.citywine shop.net.au; Mon–Fri 7am–late, Sat–Sun 9am–late; $$
You can choose from a selection of 3,000 bottles here (both New and Old World), and a generous number of these are also available by the glass. The menu plays second fiddle to the wine, but still deserves an encore when it comes to both flavour and presentation. In the morning, coffee and pastries reign supreme.

② THE EUROPEAN
161 Spring Steet; tel: 9654 0811; www.theeuropean. com.au; daily 7.30am–3.30am; $$$
Run by the same crew as the City Wine Shop, this elegant café-restaurant has been serving European dishes and drops for over a decade. The menu is more extensive and sophisticated than that of its neighbour, but the same laid-back European ambience features. Breakfasts are excellent and great value.

③ CELLAR BAR
80 Bourke Street; tel: 9662 1811; http://grossiflorentino. com; Mon–Sat 7.30am–late; $
This classic *enoteca* has a *simpatico* menu and atmosphere. You can enjoy a simple breakfast, graze on antipasto, tuck into a rustic pasta or risotto or just relax over a coffee or glass of *vino*. The scene at the outdoor tables can be fascinating to watch.

Above from left:
Queen Victoria
Market; the Royal
Arcade.

is often described as the world's first narrative film. The department later expanded into the Limelight Film Studios, the first major film production unit in Australia. The building still functions as the Salvation Army's southern territorial headquarters.

Further down the street, on the northeastern corner of Bourke and Exhibitions streets, is the elegant **Former London Chartered Bank**, erected in 1870–1.

EXHIBITION STREET TO SWANSTON STREET

More Front than Myer's
Arriving penniless from Russia in 1899, Simcha Baevski (later Sidney Myer) worked in a Flinders Lane clothing business. It didn't take long for his entrepreneurial skills to emerge, and after working as a hawker he set up drapery shops in Bendigo and Melbourne before opening his magnificent self-titled emporium in the city. His store – and achievement – was so huge that locals use the saying 'more front than Myer's' to describe cheeky confidence.

This stretch of Bourke Street has been bastardised over the last fifty years, and few remnants of its illustrious past remain. After crossing Exhibition Street, continue downhill and you will soon see the Allans Music Building on the left, once the home of the **Eastern Arcade** ❾. Look up and you will see the arcade's exotic Moorish façade, which dates from 1894.

Former Bank of NSW

Further on, over Russell Street and on the opposite side of the road at nos 190–192, is the **Former Bank of NSW Building** ❿, which was built in 1931. Its over-the-top decoration reflects the craze at that time for all things Egyptian, a phenomenon inspired by Howard Carter's 1922 discovery of Tutankhamun's tomb in

the Valley of the Kings at Luxor. Note the curved top parapet formed of stylised papyrus fronds.

The stern bulk of the **Commonwealth Bank Building** ⓫ on the southern side of the street at nos 219–225 stands in total contrast. Built in 1940, this is the best example of an Art Deco skyscraper in the city but has none of the glamour of its neighbour.

BOURKE STREET MALL

The block between Swanston and Elizabeth streets has been the mercantile heart of the city since the early 20th century, when the Myer and Buckley & Nunn emporiums opened. Back then, ladies from the suburbs donned hat, gloves and handbag and travelled by tram to these city stores in order to enjoy a day marvelling at the modern merchandise on offer. And although the suburban mall is as common here in Melbourne as it is in Middle America, many locals still emulate their parents and grandparents and make regular pilgrimages into Myer and DJs for a big day out.

David Jones

Melbourne's best department store (commonly known as 'DJs') occupies three buildings on opposite sides of the mall. On the southern side of the mall is the **David Jones Men's Store** ⓬ (www.davidjones.com.au), formerly

the G.J. Coles Department Store, a striking pink Art Deco building built between 1929–38. On the northern side is the **Former Buckley & Nunn Men's Store 🔞**, a fabulous Jazz Moderne building from 1933, featuring a façade of glossy black tiles, chrome zigzag detailing and coloured tilework details. Next to it is an elegant Edwardian building opened in 1912 as the flagship **Buckley & Nunn Emporium 🔞**. These two buildings now house the **David Jones Women's Store**.

Myer

There's a certain amount of truth to this store's advertising boast that 'Myer is Melbourne', as it has been a favoured shopping destination for Melburnians from as early as 1911. Established by Sidney Myer *(see margin, left)*, the **Myer Emporium 🔞** (www.myer.com.au) colonised large tracts of Bourke and Lonsdale streets in the 1920s and 1930s, with the construction of handsome buildings such as this Commercial Gothic structure at nos 314–336. Lauded as a 'Cathedral of Commerce' when it was opened in 1933, this building once sported a stylish Art Deco fitout, traces of which still remain. The best of these is the Myer Mural Hall, which is adorned with huge chandeliers and a mural cycle entitled *Females Through the Ages* by local artist Napier Waller.

Royal Arcade

Across the mall is the oldest surviving shopping arcade in Australia. **Royal Arcade 🔞** is still looking spruce, courtesy of a costly and sympathetic

Queen Victoria Market

A short detour north along Elizabeth Street will bring you to the historic Queen Victoria Market (corner Elizabeth and Victoria streets; tel: 9320 5835; www.qvm.com.au; Tue and Thur 6am–2pm, Fri 6am–5pm, Sat 6am–3pm, Sun 9am–4pm; guided tours at 10am–noon on Tue, Thur, Fri and Sat; charge for tour), where generations of Melburnians have done their weekly produce shopping. A stroll around the bustling deli hall, fruit and vegetable sheds, and fish and meat hall reinforces the fact that Australia has a range and quality of foodstuffs unparalleled in the world – if you can't find an in-season product here, you are unlikely to find it anywhere. It is always fascinating to notice the ethnicity of the market's stallholders – this has been a reflection of immigration trends to the city ever since its establishment in 1878.

Above from left:
Gog guards the Royal Arcade clock along with Magog; GPO shopping centre on Bourke Street Mall; Flinders Street Station; Australia Day on Federation Square.

recent restoration. Architect Charles Webb referenced the grand arcades of London and Paris in this 1869–71 confection, endowing it with a long glassed roof and arched windowed storerooms above the 28 shops. Original tenants included the Royal Turkish Baths (closed in 1927) and prominent clockmaker and jeweller Thomas Gaunt & Co., who made the large clock at the southern end of the arcade. The clock is guarded either side by Gog and Magog, figures of myth-

ical British giants copied from larger effigies at London's Guildhall.

GPO

The **Former General Post Office** ⑰ on the northeastern corner of Bourke and Elizabeth streets surrendered its philatelic and mail function in 2001 and now houses **GPO** (tel: 9663 0066; www.melbournesgpo.com; Mon–Sat 10am–6pm, Fri until 8pm, Sun 11am–5pm), an upmarket shopping mall dominated by fashion retailers. Built in stages between 1861–1907, the building's riot of columns, elevated open arcade and visually prominent clocktower make it a true city landmark. Shops worth checking out include designer boutiques such as Wayne Cooper, Leona Edmiston, Lisa Ho, and the **ABC Shop** on the mezzanine; the latter sells merchandise associated with the ABC television and radio channels.

Refreshment Options

By this stage you are probably ready for something to eat or drink. If you are feeling peckish, turn left into Elizabeth Street and then right into Little Collins Street. Slightly up the hill on the right is tiny Gills Lane, home to the casually chic **Gills Diner**, see ⑪④. Alternatively, you can veer right into Elizabeth Street, right again into Little Bourke Street and left into dingy Driver Lane to reach **MOO** (Money Order Office, see ⑪⑤), a perfect spot for a leisurely early-evening drink.

Food and Drink 🍴

④ GILLS DINER
Rear 360 Little Collins Street; tel: 9670 7214; Mon–Fri noon–3pm, Tue–Sat 5–10pm; $$
One of the in-crowd's favourite city eateries, Gills Diner serves simple but delicious European-derived dishes at extremely reasonable prices. You will find it behind the Commercial Bakery.

⑤ MOO
Basement 318 Little Bourke Street; tel: 9639 3020; www.moneyorderoffice.com.au; Tue–Fri noon–3pm, Tue–Sat 6–11pm, bar Tue–Sat 5pm–late; $$$
Imagine a Baroque boudoir crossed with a London gentlemen's club and you get an idea of what Money Order Office (MOO) is like. A subterranean restaurant-bar with mood lighting and an exceptionally fine wine list, it is beloved by businessmen on the make and fashionistas from the GPO.

SWANSTON STREET

Straight as an arrow and replete with history, this major boulevard is home to civic monuments and treasures, including Flinders Street Station, Federation Square, Melbourne Town Hall and the State Library of Victoria. Take a detour into Chinatown and finish off with a dip in the City Baths.

Melbourne-born comedian Barry Humphries (of Dame Edna Everage fame) once quipped that Swanston Street was topped and tailed by the city's two most sacred sites: the Shrine of Remembrance and the Carlton and United Brewery. The brewery is long gone from its former home, but the shrine still stands majestic at the southern approach, and the street itself remains one of the city's best-known thoroughfares, home to important civic and commercial buildings.

Swanston Street was an important component of Robert Hoddle's 1837 layout of the future town of Melbourne, and today it is a major tram route connecting the inner north with suburbs on the southern side of the Yarra and around Port Phillip Bay. It is blocked to cars during the day, which makes it perfect for perambulation, although pedestrians should walk on the footpaths (sidewalks) rather than on the road, which carries a steady stream of bicycles and trams. As you walk, keep an eye out for street art, including the much-loved book sculpture in front of the State Library.

DISTANCE 2.5km (1½ miles)

TIME A half day

START Flinders Street Railway Station

END Melbourne City Baths

POINTS TO NOTE

Note that the NGV Australia is closed on Mondays. Don't forget to bring your swimming things if you wish to end the walk with a dip.

FLINDERS STREET RAILWAY STATION

Meeting friends 'under the clocks' at **Flinders Street Railway Station ❶** is a long and proud Melburnian tradition, so it is appropriate to start this walk here. The banded-brick-and-render façade and copper dome of the station building have dominated the southern gateway to the city since 1910. The stained-glass windows, pressed metalwork, zinc cladding and open-air platforms overlooking the Yarra River are architecturally distinctive, but it is the famous row of clocks at the main entrance that draws most attention.

FEDERATION SQUARE

Built to commemorate the centenary of Australia's Federation in 2001, the entertainment and cultural hub of **Federation Square ②** is situated opposite the station. Its dynamic design was inspired by Melbourne's arcades and lanes, and the building is particularly distinctive when illuminated at night. Constructing the showpiece square was a massive undertaking, politically and technically, and there are still arguments over the merits of the design. It is, however, incontrovertibly Melbourne's premier public space and has shifted the whole focus of the city.

Dubbed 'Fed Square' by locals, the cobblestone piazza is surrounded by 'shards', which house restaurants, performance spaces and three high-profile cultural institutions. The square hosts major public events, including the annual Melbourne Writers' Festival *(see p.10)*. If you need any practical information about Melbourne or Victoria, the **Melbourne Visitor Centre** (tel: 9658 9658; www.thatsmelbourne.com.au/; daily 9am–6pm) is located here, on the corner of Flinders and Swanston streets.

Centre for the Moving Image

The **Australian Centre for the Moving Image ③** (ACMI; tel: 8663 2200; www.acmi.net.au; daily 10am–6pm; charge) celebrates celluloid and other electronic arts, and has built an enthusiastic following since it opened in 2002. Impressive temporary exhibitions are staged in the screen gallery, programmes of cutting-edge film are screened in two high-tech cinemas and there is even a games lab where aficionados of the genre can test their knowledge.

The Ian Potter Centre: NGV Australia

The National Gallery of Victoria has two major locations: its flagship building in St Kilda Road *(see p.66)* and a gallery here in the square's biggest shard. The **NGV Australia ❹** (tel: 8620 2222; www.ngv.vic.gov.au; Tue–Sun 10am–5pm; permanent collection free, charge for special exhibitions) houses the institution's impressive collection of Australian art. The first galleries' indigenous art ranges from traditional bark paintings to striking modern canvases. The classic colonials and Australian Impressionists come next, and, as you progress, the pieces become more modern. Look out too for a host of unique displays on Australian photography, fashion and textiles (including dresses and hats), decorative arts (homeware and accessories), sculptures and multi-media. The NGV also hosts an impressive programme of temporary exhibitions showcasing the work of contemporary Australian artists.

ST PAUL'S CATHEDRAL

Diagonally opposite Flinders Street Railway Station is **St Paul's Anglican Cathedral ❺**, built on the site where, in March 1836, the first religious service in the new colony was held under a great gum tree. A bluestone church had been built on the site in 1852, but was replaced in 1891 by this Transitional Gothic building designed by noted English ecclesiastical architect William Butterfield. The horizontally banded stone interior, organ, stained-glass windows, Venetian glass mosaics and blackwood furniture are all worth closer inspection. The cathedral's organ was imported from England and is acknowledged as the finest surviving work of T. C. Lewis, the esteemed 19th-century organ builder.

YOUNG AND JACKSON

Opposite, on the northwestern corner of Swanston and Flinders streets, is one of Australia's most famous pubs, the unassuming but splendidly sited **Young and Jackson Hotel ❻** (tel: 9650 3884; www.youngandjackson.com.au; Mon–Thur 10am–midnight, Fri 10am–3am, Sat 9am–3am, Sun 9am–midnight). The three-storey bluestone building was constructed in 1853, and its upstairs dining room is home to Jules Lefebvre's beautiful 1875 nude *Chloe*, which was hung in 1908 and has shocked strait-laced members of the community ever since.

FLINDERS LANE

Walk north and cross Flinders Lane, once the city's garment district. The names of laneways and buildings here, such as Manchester Lane ('manchester' is an Australian term used for household linen or cotton goods), pay

Above from far left: cobblestone piazza of Fed Square; NGV Australia; stained glass at St Paul's; the famous Aussie pub.

Below: home to the NGV Australia, the Ian Potter Centre is visually striking in its own right.

Above from left:
Melbourne Town Hall;
Chinese Museum.

tribute to the businesses that thrived in this district from the 1920s to the 1960s; many of Victoria's richest family dynasties made their fortunes here. These days it features a liberal sprinkling of commercial art galleries, glam boutiques and bustling cafés.

Just off Flinders Lane are a couple of laneways – the cobbled bluestone Degraves Street and the narrow Centre Place – lined with small but vibrant eateries and bars.

If you detour left along Flinders Lane, consider stopping for breakfast or coffee at **Journal**, see ⑪①; if it is

Below: Manchester Unity Building.

later in the day, lunch at **Journal Canteen**, see ⑪②, is a great option.

Heading to the right will take you up the hill to **Anna Schwartz Gallery** at no. 185, home to the most impressive stable of contemporary artists in the city. Next door at no. 181 is **Christine**, beloved by fashionistas for its gorgeous accessories and clothes. Near the top of Flinders Lane is fashionable bar-café-eatery **Cumulus Inc.**, see ⑪③.

MELBOURNE TOWN HALL

Back on Swanston Street, walk one block until you reach Collins Street. The corner here is presided over by the imposing **Melbourne Town Hall** ❼, designed in the French Second Empire style by architect Joseph Reed, who was responsible for many of Melbourne's grand 19th-century civic buildings. Completed in 1870, it was a popular venue for public meetings in its early years, and still hosts heated debates in its council chambers.

Inside the Town Hall is the tiny **City Gallery** (Mon 10am–2pm, Tue–Thur 11am–6pm, Fri 11am–6.30pm, Sat 10am–4pm; free), which hosts a changing programme of consistently fascinating exhibitions about Melbourne's cultural, historical and artistic life. You will find it adjoining the **Half-tix box office** *(see p.20)*.

Opposite is the **Manchester Unity Building** ❽, featuring a soaring vertical design inspired by Chicago's Tribune

Building. Constructed in 1932 at the height of the Great Depression, the 11-storey 'Gothic-Deco' building was the work of noted architect Marcus Barlow. Newspapers of the time lauded it as a striking testament to the city's modernity and a vote of commercial confidence in its future. The 1938 **Century Building**, at the end of the same block, was also designed by Barlow.

Crossing Little Collins Street, look right (east) to see the attractive energy-conserving shutters of the **CH2 Building** *(see margin, right)*.

CHINATOWN

Continue north past Bourke Street. The next narrow cross street is Little Bourke Street, home to Melbourne's **Chinatown ❾**. The stretch between Swanston and Springs streets is frantically busy on Sundays, when a swathe of restaurants serve *yum cha* (dim sum). Aside from food, there are also several hip bars in Chinatown that are packed cheek by jowl on weekends.

Cantonese-speaking Chinese immigrants arrived in great numbers during the 1850s, hopeful of making fortunes in the colony they described as 'New Gold Mountain'. After periods of back-breaking work on the goldfields, they came to this part of town for some R & R, eating, gambling and smoking opium with their fellow countrymen. Benevolent societies established premises here, including the still-functioning **Sam Yup Society** (now Nam Poon Shoong) at nos 200–202. These societies were often supported by wealthy merchants and community leaders such as Low Kong Meng, who built the wedding cake-like **Sun Kum Lee Trading Company Building** at nos 112–114 in 1887–8 as a residence and business warehouse.

If you are keen to find out more about the history of the Chinese in Melbourne, consider popping into the **Chinese Museum ❿** (22 Cohen Place; tel: 9662 2888; www.chinesemuseum.com.au; daily 10am–5pm; charge).

Eco-Friendly Building
The innovative CH2 Building was designed to be the most environmentally sustainable 'green' office block in Australia. Completed in 2007, its passive energy systems have reduced its energy consumption by 87 percent, and its ability to harvest water from a nearby main sewer and recycle it within the building has cut mains water use by 70 percent.

Food and Drink

① **JOURNAL**
Shop 1, 253 Flinders Lane; tel: 9650 4399; Mon–Fri 7am–9pm, Sat–Sun 7am–6pm; $
The soaring ceilings, huge shared benches and hip vibe of this much-loved café make it a seductive pitstop at any time of the day. It's known for good coffee, crunchy bruschetta and attitude-free waiters.

② **JOURNAL CANTEEN**
Level 1, 253 Flinders Lane; tel: 9650 4399; Mon–Fri noon–3.45pm; $
Upstairs from Journal, this casual eatery is also known as Rosa's Kitchen in honour of its Sicilian chef. Seasonal produce dominates the daily menu and simplicity is the rule of thumb – the antipasto plate is a delight, the pasta dish is always al dente and the cannoli are to die for.

③ **CUMULUS INC.**
45 Flinders Lane; tel: 9650 1445; www.cumulusinc.com.au; Mon–Fri 7am–11pm, Sat–Sun 8am–11pm; $$
Über-fashionable Cumulus Inc. lives up to its hype. You can wander in for a leisurely breakfast, join the local gallery set for lunch or queue for a dinner table. The kitchen is headed by one of Melbourne's best chefs, Andrew McConnell.

Above from left:
La Trobe Reading Room in the State Library; La Mama Theatre in Melbourne's Little Italy.

Below: old and modern RMIT University façades.

STATE LIBRARY OF VICTORIA

Back on Swanston Street, continue north. Cross Lonsdale Street, walk past the **QV Centre**, a block-sized shopping complex, and you will soon come to the forecourt of the magnificent **State Library of Victoria ⑪** (328 Swanston Street; tel: 8664 7000; www.slv.vic.gov.au; Mon–Thur 10am– 9pm, Fri–Sun 10am–6pm; free).

The library was established by Lieutenant-Governor Charles Joseph La Trobe and Supreme Court judge Redmond Barry to counterbalance the upheaval of the gold rush by bringing culture, stability and an ethos of civic virtue to the colony. It was opened in stages from the mid- 19th century, and underwent a major renovation from the late 1980s to 2003. Don't miss the magnificent domed Reading Room, which dates from 1913, and the classically elegant Queen's Hall, from 1856. Items from the library's permanent collection (including Ned Kelly's suit of armour; *see margin, right*) are on display in the Dome Galleries, while temporary exhibitions are staged in the Cowen and Keith Murdoch galleries. The library's excellent café, **Mr Tulk**, see ⑪④, is a great spot for lunch.

RMIT UNIVERSITY

North of the library, across La Trobe Street, is **RMIT University ⑫**, established in 1887 as the Working Men's College. The university has a highly regarded architecture school, and over recent years has commissioned and constructed a number of architecturally significant buildings and urban design interventions on campus. These include Ashton Raggatt McDougall's bizarre 1992–5 addition to historic **Storey Hall** and Edmond & Corrigan's whimsical **Building 8**, a Postmodernist tour de force that dominates the university's Swanston Street frontage.

MELBOURNE CITY BATHS

Continue walking a bit further; across Franklin Street are the **Melbourne City Baths ⑬** (420 Swanston Street; tel: 9663 5888; Mon–Thur 6am– 10pm, Fri 6am–8pm, Sat–Sun 8am– 6pm; charge), with a public swimming pool, spa, sauna and gymnasium. Public baths were first built on this site in 1858, but the present red-brick Edwardian building dates from 1904.

Food and Drink 🍴

④ MR TULK
Corner of Swanston and La Trobe streets; tel: 8660 5700; Mon–Thur 7am–5pm, Fri 7am–9pm, Sat 9am–4pm; $
This casual café was named after Augustus Henry Tulk, the State Library's first chief librarian. Bookworms and blow-ins love its simple but stylish decor and keenly priced menu. Check the daily specials – they are consistently good.

CARLTON AND PARKVILLE

This vibrant suburb north of the city centre has played host to newly arrived migrants and student bohemians since the 1850s. En route to the cafés of 'Little Italy', discover the story of Ned Kelly, relax in the pretty Carlton Gardens and explore Australia's natural history at the Melbourne Museum.

Christened in 1852, when the *Government Gazette* advertised land for sale in 'Carlton Gardens' on the northern edge of the fledgling colonial settlement, Carlton has long been characterised by its Victorian buildings and wonderful gardens, squares, parks and reserves. Its wide tree-lined boulevards were built as extensions of William Hoddle's city grid and were soon populated by handsome buildings adorned with decorative iron lace and stone carvings.

Bohemian Suburb

In 1853 Melbourne University was established on its western border, endowing the suburb with a bohemian flavour that it retains to this day. The theatres, cafés and bookshops along Lygon Street have been frequented by generations of artists, writers, students and academics, who mingled with wave upon wave of newly arrived migrants attracted by the area's cheap housing stock and proximity to the city. Today, it is the first port of call of many migrants from Africa and Asia, who live in high-rise 1960s public housing.

DISTANCE 4.5km (2¾ miles)
TIME A full day
START Old Melbourne Gaol
END Enoteca Vino Bar
POINTS TO NOTE
Do this tour on a Saturday if you intend to watch the child-friendly play *Such a Life* at the Old Melbourne Gaol. Note also that you should arrange a tour in advance if you wish to visit the Trades Hall and/or the Royal Exhibition Building.
You can access Melbourne Zoo in Parkville by tram no. 55 from Elizabeth Street (Melbourne Zoo/Royal Park stop) or by train from Flinders Street Station on the Upfield or Gowrie lines (Royal Park stop).

OLD MELBOURNE GAOL

Begin at the **Old Melbourne Gaol** ❶ (near corner of Russell and Victoria streets; tel: 8663 7228; www.oldmelbournegoal.com.au; daily 9.30am–5pm; charge). Fascinating and forbid-

---

Ned Kelly
One of the greatest Australian icons is the daring bushranger Ned Kelly, executed for murder in 1880 at the Old Melbourne Gaol. The protective suit of home-made iron armour that this antihero wore during his famous last stand against police troopers at Glenrowan is on display in the Dome Galleries at the State Library.

Above: Old Melbourne Gaol.

ding in equal measure, this bluestone gaol dates from 1852 and is part of a large complex that comprised the gaol buildings, city watch house, magistrate's court and police headquarters. The gaol was closed in 1929, superseded by a larger, more modern facility in the northern suburb of Coburg. Macabre exhibits here include death masks of well-known criminals, such as the infamous bushranger Ned Kelly *(see margin, p.47)*, and plenty of photographic panels relating the histories and crimes of former inmates. You can also see the scaffold on which Kelly and 134 other miscreants were hanged.

If you would like to learn about the life and death of Ned Kelly, the play *Such a Life* is performed every Saturday at 12.30pm and 2pm. Included in the admission price, this one-hour performance is a hit with children and adults alike.

Crime and Justice Experience

The National Trust, which runs the gaol as a tourist attraction, offers a 'Crime and Justice Experience', including access to the gaol and its exhibits, plus a tour of the former **City Watch House ❷** in which visitors have the arrest process (body searches, mugshots, etc) explained to them by an actor masquerading as a police sergeant. During school holidays you can also visit the adjoining **Old Magistrate's Court**, a grand building where many of Victoria's most notorious criminals were convicted of and sentenced for their crimes. Both tours are included in the gaol's entrance charge.

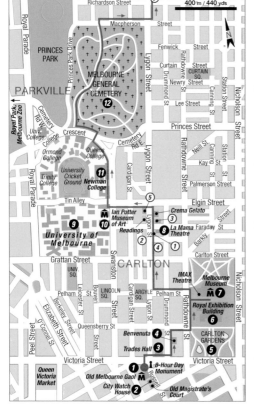

TRADES HALL

Just across from the gaol entrance, on a small traffic island, is a pink granite **monument** paying tribute to the fact that an eight-hour working day was

introduced in Victoria in 1856, decades before it was attained elsewhere in the world. The demand for eight hours' labour, eight hours' recreation and eight hours' rest was the international labour movement's response to the long hours and poor working conditions that characterised the Industrial Revolution.

Diagonally across from the monument, in Carlton proper (which officially starts on the northern side of Victoria Street), is the imposing **Trades Hall** ❸ (corner Lygon and Victoria streets; tel: 9659 3511; email: info@vthc.org.au; guided tours by prior appointment Mon–Fri 9am–5pm; charge). This building dates from 1875 and replaced an earlier, more modest, structure that was frequented predominantly by stonemasons (who led the Eight-Hour Movement). The guided tour shows you the old council chamber, murals commemorating pioneers of the local labour movement and the building's famous bullet-ridden wall *(see margin, right)*.

DRUMMOND STREET

Exiting Trades Hall, walk east up busy Victoria Street and turn at the first street to the left. You have now entered Drummond Street, one of Carlton's premier addresses. In the late 19th and early 20th centuries a large and prosperous community of Jewish immigrants from Eastern Europe settled in the gracious two-storeyed terrace houses here and ran businesses on Lygon Street. Most of these Jewish residents moved south of the Yarra River in the 1950s, surrendering the street and suburb to a post-war wave of immigrants dominated by Italians.

To the right, look out for the over-the-top façade of **Benvenuta** ❹, a Baroque-style mansion at no. 48. Built in 1892–93 by the wealthy widow of a Jewish arms dealer and generally shady character named Henry Abrahams, this Drummond Street mansion has a colourful history, having functioned as an Italian Club, brothel and now a university hall of residence.

Reaching Queensberry Street, turn right and you will see Carlton Gardens directly ahead, dominated by the imposing façade and dome of the Royal Exhibition Building.

Trades Hall Murder

In 1915 Police Constable David McGrath was shot to death on the bluestone staircase inside Trades Hall after investigating a late-night break-in. John Jackson, who was found guilty of the murder, was the last man to be hanged at the Old Melbourne Gaol.

Below: the capture of Ned Kelly.

Food and Drink

① CARLTON ESPRESSO
326 Lygon Street, Carlton; tel: 9347 8482;
Mon–Sat 7am–9.30pm, Sun 8am–9pm; $
The scene here is effortlessly stylish and quintessentially Carlton. Regulars congregate at the streetside tables to discuss soccer results and the relative merits and demerits of the Ferrari Scuderia Spider over excellent coffee, pizza slices and panini.

② LYGON FOOD STORE
263 Lygon Street, Carlton; tel: 9347 6279; www.lygonfood store.com.au; Mon–Sat 7am–5pm, Sun 8am–5pm; $
Many Melburnians had their first memorable taste of grainy Grana Padano or garlicky salami at this Melbourne institution. You can enjoy a top-quality coffee, focaccia or panini sitting indoors or outdoors, or opt to take your goodies with you.

③ BRUNETTI CAFFÈ
194–204 Faraday Street, Carlton; tel: 9347 2801; www.brunetti.com.au; Sun–Thur 6am–11pm, Fri–Sat 6am–midnight; $
The *principessa* of the Lygon Street café scene, Brunetti is a true phenomenon. Melburnians travel from every corner of the city to sample its peerless pastries, decadent cakes and consistently good coffee.

④ DONNINI'S RESTAURANT
320 Lygon Street, Carlton; tel: 9347 3128; daily noon–10pm; $$
You will feel as if you have been transported to Antonio Carluccio's home kitchen (or maybe that of your *nonna*) when you sample the excellent home-made pasta on offer at this bustling trattoria. This is comfort food Italian-style – no wonder it's perennially popular.

⑤ JIMMY WATSON'S WINE BAR
333 Lygon Street, Carlton; tel: 9347 3985; Mon 10.30am–6pm, Tue–Sat 11am–late, Sun 10.30am–3.30pm; $$
Generations of students and academics from Melbourne University have skipped afternoon classes to linger over a tipple or two at Watson's. There are tables in the rear courtyard, but most patrons prefer the minimal interior, designed by revered local architect Robin Boyd in 1962.

CARLTON GARDENS

In the early years of the settlement, visiting **Carlton Gardens ⑤** could be fraught with danger. Gangs of local boys (known as larrikins) regularly destroyed its plantings of trees and flowers during rowdy games of football, and ladies enjoying a quiet perambulation were often threatened by unruly flocks of goats. All this changed during preparations for the Melbourne International Exhibition of 1880–1, when avenues of deciduous trees, huge flower beds, grand fountains, ponds and ceremonial paths were introduced. Nowadays, each April the gardens host the wildly popular Melbourne International Flower and Garden Show.

Royal Exhibition Building

Australia has a wealth of natural landscapes and Aboriginal cultural sites on Unesco's World Heritage List, but only two built structures have been granted this honour: Sydney's Opera House and Melbourne's **Royal Exhibition Building ⑥** (9 Nicholson Street; tel: 131 102; www.museum. vic.gov.au/reb; guided tours most days at 2pm, must be booked in advance on the morning of the tour; charge). The huge scale and classical design of this exhibition pavilion reflected the boundless energy, optimism and wealth of gold rush-era Victoria. Sited in the centre of Carlton Gardens and completed in 1880, it played host to

the Melbourne International Exhibition, the Centennial International Exhibition of 1888 and the opening of Federal Parliament in 1901. The stunning interior, featuring the 1901 colour scheme and soaring ceilings, has been meticulously restored.

Melbourne Museum

Standing in stark contrast to the ornate Victorian splendour of the Royal Exhibition Building is the sleek and contemporary **Melbourne Museum** ❼ (Nicholson Street; tel: 131 102; www. museumvictoria.com.au/melbourne museum; daily 10am–5pm; charge), designed by internationally acclaimed Melbourne-based architects Denton Corker Marshall. Located immediately north of the Royal Exhibition Building, this multimedia institution has eight galleries aimed at giving visitors an insight into Australia's natural environment, culture and history. Highlights include walking through a living rainforest and learning about local Aboriginal culture at the Bunjilaka Cultural Centre. The museum's most popular exhibit introduces visitors to the famous racehorse Phar Lap, an ugly but tenacious steed who won innumerable races in the midst of the Great Depression and allowed Australians to forget – if only for the length of a race – how difficult life had become.

Film fans can watch 3D films at the IMAX Melbourne Museum (www. imaxmelbourne.com.au) too.

LITTLE ITALY

Exit the museum and turn to the right, crossing Rathdowne Street and following Pelham Street to the city's Italian quarter, Lygon Street. This busy shopping and entertainment strip is lined with plane trees and streetside cafés. Many of these cafés are shameless tourist traps serving indifferent coffee and even worse food, but scattered among them are a number of gems.

Refreshment Options

Walk north past the tourist restaurants housed in handsome Victorian terraces and cross Grattan Street. This is the heart of Little Italy, where you can enjoy a coffee and snack at **Carlton Espresso**, see ⑪①, the **Lygon Food Store**, see ⑪②, or **Brunetti**, see ⑪③. If you fancy a more substantial lunch, head to **Donnini's**, see ⑪④, for pasta, or **Jimmy Watson's Wine Bar**, see ⑪⑤, for a plate of antipasto and a glass of excellent Australian wine.

On and directly surrounding this stretch of Lygon Street you will find the city's best independent bookshop, **Readings** (www.readings.com.au) at no. 309, and the *delizioso* ice-cream parlour **Crema Gelato** at no. 342. Just to the east on Faraday Street, you will see the ramshackle but much-loved **La Mama Theatre** (www.lamama.com.au) ❽, one of the few remnants of the suburb's history as the epicentre of Australia's alternative theatre scene in the 1970s.

Above from far left: Carlton Gardens and the Royal Exhibition Building; you will find plenty of pizza on Lygon Street.

Below: exhibits at Melbourne Museum.

UNIVERSITY
OF MELBOURNE

Turn left at Elgin Street, walk for two blocks and you will come to the **University of Melbourne ❾**, which straddles the suburbs of Carlton and Parkville. Within its leafy grounds a number of charming Gothic-style sandstone buildings from the 19th

Below: Newman College Chapel at Melbourne University.

century are scattered among stern curtain-walled 1950s blocks and unfortunate 1970s Brutalist interventions.

Ian Potter Museum of Art

There are a number of museums and galleries within the university; most impressive is the **Ian Potter Museum of Art ❿** (corner Swanston and Elgin streets; tel: 8344 5148; www.art-museum.unimelb.edu.au; Tue–Fri 10am–5pm, Sat–Sun noon–5pm, closed late Dec–mid-Jan; free). The cutting-edge credentials of the gallery are heralded by Christine O'Loughlin's *Cultural Rubble* sculpture installation (1993), which adorns the main façade of the building, and the exhibition programme in the main downstairs galleries is consistently impressive. Upstairs galleries play host to changing exhibitions of items from the university's enormous art collection, including its world-class classical and archaeology collections.

College Crescent

Leaving the museum, walk north along College Crescent past the main strip of university residential colleges. These include the stunningly original **Newman College ⓫**, designed by American architect Walter Burley Griffin and constructed between 1915–18. Griffin and his architect wife Marion Mahony came to Australia after winning an international competition to design Australia's capital, Canberra.

MELBOURNE GENERAL CEMETERY

Crossing at the huge roundabout, you will come to the perimeter fence of the **Melbourne General Cemetery** ⓬ (tel: 9349 3014; www.necropolis.net.au/melbournegeneral; daily 9am–5pm), which has been in operation since 1853. Many of the first colonists are buried here, and a wander around the graves shows how short many lives were in those harsh early days. After entering through the main gate, walk through the rose garden on the right and you will eventually see a large and sombre monument to explorers Robert O'Hara Burke and William John Wills of the Victoria Exploring Expedition, who died of exhaustion at Cooper's Creek, Queensland, in 1861. They and two others were returning from crossing the continent from south to north and mapping its hitherto unexplored interior. The expedition had set off from nearby **Royal Park** *(see right)* on 20 August 1860, farewelled by a crowd of 15,000.

Returning to Entrance Avenue, proceed north. Among others, you will pass the graves of Prime Minster James Henry Scullin (1876–1953) and billiards player Walter Lindrum (1898–1960), who won the World Professional Billiards Championship in 1933 and held the title until 1950. Lindrum's famously laconic sense of humour is reflected in the epitaph on his billiard table-shaped gravestone: 'It's queer how folks you'd never miss it seems can always stay/When folks you love and want so much must always pass away.'

Exiting the cemetery from the northern gate on Macpherson Street, turn right and walk down to Lygon Street. Turn left and walk north for a block. Across the road is **Enoteca Vino Bar**, see ⓘⓖ, the perfect spot for an *aperitivo* or early dinner.

Above from far left: Old Quad at the University of Melbourne; gravestones at Melbourne General Cemetery.

Food and Drink

⑥ ENOTECA VINO BAR

920 Lygon Street, North Carlton; tel: 9389 7070; www.enoteca.com.au; Tue–Sat 9am–late, Sun 9am–4pm; $$$
Behind the ugly façade of this former neighbourhood pub is a stylish space functioning as a bar-café-restaurant-*providore*. As befits its location, the wine, food and provisions are exclusively Italian, showcasing regional varietals, classic dishes and artisan-made products.

Melbourne Zoo

Sprawling Royal Park, west of the cemetery, is where the indigenous Wurundjeri people once camped and held huge tribal gatherings called *corroborees*. In the middle of the park is the Melbourne Zoo (Elliott Avenue; tel: 9285 9300; www.zoo.org.au/Melbourne; daily 9am–5pm; charge), one of the state's most popular tourist attractions. Opened in 1862, it is the oldest zoo in Australia and the third-oldest in the world. It has a renowned conservation research programme and over 300 species of animals, all of which are housed in different bioclimatic (habitat) zones. If you have never before encountered local furry friends, such as kangaroos, koalas, emus, wombats and platypuses, this is an ideal place to do so.

FITZROY

Melbourne's first suburb, this enclave on the city fringe has a down-to-earth ambience and inclusive air befitting its working-class history. Explore the funky shopping and entertainment strips of Brunswick and Gertrude streets.

DISTANCE 2.5km (1½ miles)
TIME A half day
START Tram Engine House
END Centre for Contemporary Photography
POINTS TO NOTE
After finishing this walk, you could catch tram no. 112 south along Brunswick Street to the city centre and then on to St Kilda (walk 11). Alternatively, combine the tour with an afternoon in Carlton (walk 4).

First subdivided in 1839, the suburb now known as Fitzroy was initially part of an area called New Town, which stretched from the northeastern corner of the City of Melbourne down towards the flats of the Yarra River at Collingwood. It was proclaimed an independent municipality in 1878.

Arty Enclave

Famous for its shabby-chic main artery, Brunswick Street, the suburb has long been the haunt of students, activists, musicians, artists and the Aboriginal community. Melbourne's major alternative arts festival, the Melbourne Fringe *(see p.21)*, was born here in 1982; and longstanding incubator of the arts, **Gertrude Contemporary Art Spaces** (200 Gertrude Street; tel: 9419 3406; www.gertrude.org.au), arrived on the scene the following year.

Nowadays, high rents have forced many longstanding residents to relocate north to Brunswick or west to Footscray and Yarraville, but these exiles are inevitably lured back at weekends, when they prop up the bar at favourite drinking dens, contemplate the cutting-edge at gallery openings or linger over lattes in laidback cafés.

Koorie Culture

Fitzroy has always been a cultural hub for Melbourne's Koorie (Aboriginal) community. Favoured post-World War II meeting places were the Builder's Arms Hotel and Fitzroy Gym on Gertrude Street and the Aboriginal Church of Christ in Gore Street. Today, the hubs are the Aboriginal Health Service at 186 Nicholson Street and the streets around Safeway supermarket in Collingwood.

GERTRUDE STREET

Start at the **Former Cable Tram Engine House ❶**, an elegant Italianate building on the corner of Nicholson and Gertrude streets, opposite the Royal Exhibition Building *(see p.50)*. Built in 1886–7 for the Melbourne Tramway Trust, this was an important element of Melbourne's famous cable tramway system, which was the largest in the world. The engine house ceased to function in 1940, when the city's tram system was electrified.

On the opposite corner, facing the Melbourne Museum *(see p.51)*, is elegant **Royal Terrace ❷**, a row of ten three-storey bluestone terrace houses dating from 1854. A short way east at nos 64–78 is **Glass Terrace ❸**, thought to be the oldest surviving terrace building in Melbourne. It was built between 1854–6 for Irish-born speculator and pastoralist Hugh Glass, one of the wealthiest and most influential men in the colony during the 1850s and 60s.

Boutiques and Bars

Once a seedy strip frequented by drug dealers, drunks and other down-at-heel Fitzrovians, Gertrude Street has reinvented itself in recent years. Boutiques and ateliers, such as **Cottage Industry** (no. 67), **Vixen** (no. 163) and **Crumpler** (corner of Gertrude and Smith streets), showcase wares made by local artisans and designers *(see p.18)*, while stylish bars and eateries attract both locals and visitors. The best of these are top-notch tapas bar **Añada** (no. 197), **Gertrude Street Enoteca**, see ⑪①, and **Ladro** (no. 224), home to the city's best pizzas.

Above from far left: international retailer of hip bags and backpacks, Crumpler was founded in Melbourne; Black Cat Building on Brunswick Street.

Below: Gertrude Street Enoteca.

Food and Drink 🍴

① GERTRUDE STREET ENOTECA

229 Gertrude Street; tel: 9415 8262; Mon–Fri 8am–10pm, Sat 10am–10pm; $$
They take food and wine seriously at this tiny café-cum-wine-bar, and local gastronomes return the favour. The food menu is limited, with a strong emphasis on seasonal produce and simple execution, but there's an impressive choice of wines by the glass. The coffee is excellent too, particularly when accompanied by your choice of a biscuit or slice of cake made daily on the premises.

Above from left:
watering hole on
Brunswick Street;
Centre for Contemporary Photography;
gargoyle on St
Patrick's Cathedral;
detail on a house on
Powlett Street.

BRUNSWICK STREET

Proceed north into Brunswick Street and head past the huge public-housing estate called Atherton Gardens, with its Russian Matryoshka Dolls sculpture, by Bronwen Gray, facing the street. Further along, past the popular Malaysian restaurant **Blue Chillies**, see ⑪②, is the street's signature building at nos 236–253 on the corner of Greeves Street. Built in 1888, the building's polychrome brickwork, central tower and corner turret are familiar to all Melburnians, who refer to it as the **Black Cat Building** ❹ after the casual bar (formerly a café) that occupies the corner shopfront, and is a Fitzroy institution.

Cafés and Commerce

The stretch between Greeves and Westgarth streets is where most of Brunswick Street's action plays out. Popular watering holes include the retro-cosy **Black Pearl** (no. 304), grungy **Bimbo Deluxe** (no. 376), industrial-chic **St Jude's Cellar** (nos 389–391) and vaguely louche **Polly** (no. 401). For lunch or coffee, the perennially popular choices are **Marios**, see ⑪③, and **Babka**, see ⑪④.

Stand-out shopping options include exquisite toiletries at **Kleins Perfumery** (no. 313), alternative music, zines and books at **PolyEster** (nos 330 and 387), well-priced designer jewellery at **Koko** (no. 332) and fragrant teas at **T2** (no. 340). As you walk down the street, look out for pavement mosaics and shopfront decorations. All have been created by local artists.

CONTEMPORARY PHOTOGRAPHY CENTRE

Turn east into Kerr Street and walk until you arrive at the third cross street. Here you will find the **Centre for Contemporary Photography** ❺ (CCP; 404 George Street; tel: 9417 1549; www.ccp.org.au; Wed–Fri 11am–6pm, Sat–Sun noon–5pm; free), a purpose-designed space showcasing changing exhibitions of photography and video art. Even after dark you can sample the artwork courtesy of the Projection Window.

Food and Drink

② BLUE CHILLIES
182 Brunswick Street; tel: 9417 0071; www.bluechillies.com.au; daily noon–2.30pm, Mon–Thur 6–10.30pm, Fri–Sat until 11pm, Sun until 10pm; $$
The curry *laksa* (noodle soup) here is justly famous, but alternatives such as beef *rendang* and *char kway teow* (Malaysian fried rice noodles) are equally delicious.

③ MARIOS
303 Brunswick Street; tel: 9417 3343; daily 7am–11pm; $
There is an over-abundance of cafés on Brunswick Street, but this one reigns supreme for three reasons: great coffee, all-day breakfasts and fast and friendly service.

④ BABKA
358 Brunswick Street; tel: 9416 0091; Tue–Sun 7am–7pm; $
Breakfast and Babka is a match made in heaven. Breads and pastries fresh from the oven are served with home-made jam – bliss! Queuing for a table is de rigueur.

EAST MELBOURNE

Elegant East Melbourne is in a class of its own. Its proximity to the city centre, Victorian-era streetscapes and genteel atmosphere make it an address many aspire to. This walk explores historic Eastern Hill and Fitzroy Gardens.

When the Anglican Bishop of Melbourne and his wife set up house in East Melbourne in 1853, they were the first well-connected members of society to call the suburb home. Their bluestone house, 'Bishopscourt', survives to this day on the corner of Clarendon and Gipps streets, surrounded by a score of gracious Victorian townhouses occupied by surgeons, barristers, investment bankers and arts professionals, many of whom walk to their workplaces through the historic Fitzroy Gardens. There's serious money here, but little ostentation, making it a classy contrast to the gilded suburbs south of the Yarra.

DISTANCE 1.25km (¾ mile)

TIME 3 hours

START Orica House

END Fitzroy Gardens

POINTS TO NOTE

Orica House is located between Carlton Gardens and Parliament House. This short walk could easily be combined with Bourke Street (walk 2), Carlton (walk 4) or Fitzroy (walk 5). If you decide to visit the Johnston Collection, it is essential to book at least one day in advance of your preferred visiting time.

ORICA HOUSE

Start at **Orica House ❶** on the corner of Albert and Nicholson streets, formerly known as ICI House. Designed by local architectural firm Bates Smart McCutcheon and completed in 1958, it was the first building to break the 132ft (40.2m) height limit then applied to all city buildings, and was the tallest building in Australia until 1961. A Modernist masterpiece, it features the steel frame and curtain-wall glass so beloved by European and

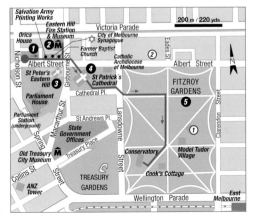

Cloud Kisser

When ICI House (now Orica House) embraced the clouds on the eastern edge of Melbourne's Central Business District, many local critics were horrified. Australian artist Norman Lindsay said that it 'represented a final triumph to modernistic art, with its slogan of death to all beauty', and went on to opine that there was 'only one finality to such abominable glass anthills and that is a bomb'.

American architects of the post-war period. The garden, water feature and fountain sculpture are all original.

EASTERN HILL

Walking east along Albert Street, you will pass the distinctive red-and-white **Salvation Army Printing Works** at nos 500–502 and the **City of Melbourne Synagogue** at nos 494–498. The synagogue was built between 1877–83, and its Renaissance Revival façade stands in almost frivolous contrast to the stern classical portico of the **Former Baptist Church** (at nos 486–492), which dates from 1863.

Fire Services Museum

A short detour left (north) up Gisbourne Street will bring you to the **Eastern Hill Fire Station ❷** on the

corner of Victoria Parade, built as a headquarters for the newly established Metropolitan Fire Brigade and opened in 1893. Sited at the highest point of the city, its 52m (171ft) tower once commanded panoramic views over Melbourne, allowing fires to be spotted.

The station now houses the **Fire Services Museum** (39 Gisborne Street; tel: 9662 2907; Thur–Fri 9am–3pm, Sun 10am–4pm; charge), with displays of fire engines and fire-fighting equipment that young children adore.

St Peter's Eastern Hill

The foundation stone for the pretty Anglican church of **St Peter's Eastern Hill ❸** on the southwestern corner of Albert and Gisborne streets was laid by Lieutenant-Governor Charles Joseph La Trobe on 18 June 1846. Parts of the church date from 1848, making it one of the few pre-gold rush buildings in central Melbourne. It has been modified many times, most recently in 1945, when a stained-glass window by artist Napier Waller was added.

St Patrick's Cathedral

Across Gisborne Street, sitting in a 2ha (5-acre) site gifted to the Catholic Church between 1848–53, is the Gothic Revival **St Patrick's Cathedral ❹**. Erected in stages from 1858 to 1940, its magnificent scale and superb detailing reflect the wealth and optimism of the young colony. Architect William Wardell's design was heavily

Food and Drink 🍴

① THE PAVILION FITZROY GARDENS

Fitzroy Gardens, Wellington Parade; tel: 9417 2544; www.thepavilionfitzroygardens.com.au; daily 9am–4pm; $
This glass pavilion nestled in the gardens is a popular spot to enjoy a casual cup of coffee or tea. You can sit indoors which has floor to ceiling windows or on the terrace.

② LE GOURMET

366 Albert Street; tel: 9419 9359; www.legourmet.com.au; Tue–Fri noon–3pm and 6–10.30pm, Sat 6–10.30pm; $$$
East Melbourne is a largely residential suburb, so restaurants and cafés are few and far between. Fortunately, this elegant eatery provides an exception to the rule. The decor is as conservative as the menu, which features well-executed French and Austrian-accented dishes.

influenced by the work of Augustus Pugin (1812–52), the visionary architect whose Gothic Revival designs and 1841 book *True Principles of Christian Architecture* changed ecclesiastical architecture in Britain for ever. The stunning stained glass was produced by workshops in Munich and Birmingham.

St Patrick's College, a Jesuit grammar school, was built behind the cathedral between 1854–61. The bluestone tower in the southeastern corner of the site is all that remains; the college was demolished in 1971 after an unsuccessful preservation campaign by the National Trust. In its place, local architectural firm Yuncken and Freeman designed a headquarters for the **Catholic Archdiocese of Melbourne**. Their innovative subterranean building features a circular courtyard and tranquil water pools fronting Albert Street.

FITZROY GARDENS

Cross Lansdowne Street to the charming **Fitzroy Gardens** ❺, laid out in the 1850s. These feature original elm trees, formal paths, sweeping lawns, statuary and a number of structures, some more felicitous than others. The Spanish Mission-style **Conservatory** is particularly attractive. Also here is **Cooks' Cottage**, the home of Captain James Cook's parents, which was transported here from Yorkshire in 1933.

In the centre of the gardens is **The Pavilion Fitzroy Gardens**, see ⑪①,

where you can enjoy a coffee or tea at the end of your walk. Alternatively, you can make your way to nearby **Le Gourmet**, see ⑪②, for a formal lunch or dinner.

Above from far left:
Fire Services Museum; Cooks' Cottage, Fitzroy Gardens.

The Johnston Collection

You might like to extend this tour by visiting the Johnston Collection (tel: 9416 2515; www.johnstoncollection.org), a house museum on Hotham Street, just to the east of Fitzroy Gardens. The legacy of antiques dealer William Robert Johnston, the collection occupies almost every room of Fairhall, a Georgian-style house dating from 1860. The museum opened in 1986, showcasing Johnston's extraordinary collection of Georgian, Regency and Louis XV furniture and decorative arts.

Because the Johnston Collection is located in a residential street (one of Melbourne's finest), it doesn't have a standard permit to operate as a public museum. To visit, you must book a place on one of the three tours that operate every weekday (10am, noon and 2.15pm) and you will be transported to the site by minibus from the foyer of the Hilton on the Park Hotel on Wellington Parade, at the southeastern corner of Fitzroy Gardens.

THE YARRA AND DOCKLANDS

Its murky appearance has led to the Yarra being described as a river flowing upside down, but the indigenous Wurundjeri people refer to it more poetically as Birrarung, the River of Mist. This waterside walk takes in world-class sports arenas, memorable Southbank views and high-class restaurants.

Water Wheels
Melbourne Water Taxis (tel: 0416 068 655; www.melbourne watertaxis.com.au; daily 9am–midnight; charge) offers on-demand services up and down the Yarra, into the Docklands and over the bay to Williamstown. It also runs a regular service between Southgate and Melbourne Park/ MCG when concerts, AFL matches or the Australian Tennis Open are held.

DISTANCE 6.5km (4 miles)
TIME A full day
START Melbourne Cricket Ground (MCG)
END NewQuay, Docklands
POINTS TO NOTE
To get to the MCG, you can walk east from the city centre, take a train to Jolimont Station (Epping or Hurstbridge lines), take tram no. 48 or 75 travelling east along Flinders Street (Jolimont Station stop 11) or take the no. 70 tram from Flinders Street (Melbourne Park stop 7C). To return, catch the free City Circle tram from Harbour Esplanade.

The Yarra

Sydneysiders tend to sneer at Melbourne's unassuming Yarra River. And when compared with their beautiful harbour, this narrow band of brown water does indeed seem to lack visual appeal and strategic importance. But further investigation will reward the visitor, as a walk along its central section is in many ways an introduction to the soul of the city. Icon after icon is dotted on its banks; a flotilla of rowboats, kayaks and water taxis battle its sometimes deadly currents; and umpteen Melburnians enjoy its sporting and recreational amenities at weekends and on summer evenings.

In 1835 John Batman's identification of fresh water above falls 10km (6 miles) from the river's mouth determined the location of the village that would become Melbourne. Soon after, Robert Hoddle aligned his grid for the city's streets with its course. Ever since, the river has been a topographic landmark, demarcating the northern and southern sides of town.

With the development of the Docklands and South Wharf precincts at the western edge of the city centre, the Yarra hopes to serve an even more strategic function, drawing together the leafy residential east and the still-industrial west, and reminding Melburnians of the maritime functions that continue to flourish in their midst.

MELBOURNE CRICKET GROUND

Australians have a unique attitude towards sport, supporting teams and individual players with an evangelical fervour rarely exhibited in the nation's churches, mosques and temples. Although each state has its signature stadium, only one has an arena that is regularly described as a sporting shrine – and that, of course, is Victoria's **Melbourne Cricket Ground ❶** (MCG; Brunton Avenue; tel: 9657 8879; www. mcg.org.au). Known to Melburnians as 'the 'G', this massive structure is home to international cricket and Australia's hugely popular home-grown football code, Australian ('Aussie') Rules. It also hosted the 1956 Olympic Games.

Aussie Rules
Australia's first football match was played in 1858 by cricketers looking for an off-season sport. Then, the game thrived on the rivalry and class differences between the suburbs and the fierce pride of the players and fans. And although the class differences may have diminished and the teams' ties to particular suburbs may have become tenuous, the power and the passion of the code remains. Weekend footy continues to be an intrinsic part of life for hundreds of thousands of Melburnians, and for many players the pinnacle of their career is an appearance at the 'G, preferably in a Grand Final *(see p.22)*.

Test Cricket
Fans of cricket are similarly devoted. Cricket has been played at the MCG since 1853, and the ground hosted the first-ever Test match in 1877. The Boxing Day Test at the 'G is world-famous, and a summer afternoon spent in the stands watching the Australian Test or one-day sides strut their stuff is a right of passage for most local men and an ever-increasing number of women.

Stadium Tours
The MCG is one of the largest stadiums in the world, with a capacity of 100,000. One-hour guided tours depart from

Above from far left: rowing on the Yarra; spectating at an AFL game at the MCG.

Left: statue of Dennis Lillee, former Australian fast bowler, at the MCG.

MELBOURNE CRICKET GROUND **61**

Above from left:
auditorium of the
State Theatre in the
Arts Centre; Feder-
ation Bells in Birra-
rung Marr; National
Sports Museum.

Gate 3 of the Olympic Stand most non-
event days between 10am and 3pm.

National Sports Museum

It is possible to purchase a ticket for the
stadium tour that includes entrance to
the **National Sports Museum** (tel:
9657 8879; www.nsm.org.au; daily
10am–5pm; charge), which is located
within the MCG's Olympic Stand.
The museum complex houses Australia's finest sporting heritage with a
collection of sports artefacts, covering
20 sporting codes.

The museum incorporates Australia's Game (tracing the history of
Australian football), Melbourne
Cricket Club Museum, and Cham-
pions: Thoroughbred Racing Gallery
(formerly Australian Racing Museum),
plus temporary exhibition areas.

MELBOURNE AND OLYMPIC PARKS

Cross the footbridge over Brunton
Avenue on the southern side of the
stadium and you will find yourself in
another sporting precinct – **Melbourne & Olympic Parks ②** (www.
mopt.com.au). Here, the **Rod Laver
and Hisense Arenas** play host to the
Australian Tennis Open *(see p.23)* and
concerts. The South Dragons basketball team has its home in Hisense
Arena and the Collingwood Football
Club (aka the Magpies) is based at the
Lexus Centre.

Situated within this sports precinct
too is the stunning **AAMI Park**
(www.aamipark.com.au), built for rec-
tangular sports. Opened in 2010, it is
the home ground of the A-League,

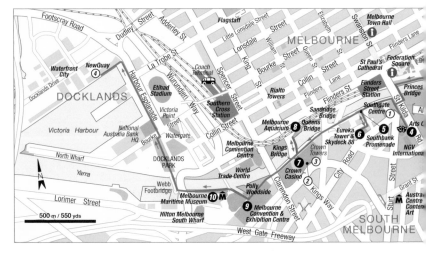

Rugby League and Rugby Union. It features a cutting-edge bioframe design with a geodesic dome roof which covers the seating area, and is designed to allow over 30,000 spectators an unobstructed view.

BIRRARUNG MARR

From the Rod Laver Arena, walk north past the tennis courts and cross the footbridge over Batman Avenue to enter **Birrarung Marr** ❸, the first major area of parkland to be created in the city for over a century. The 8.3ha (20-acre) park features indigenous flora, river views, a children's playground and the **Federation Bells**, a set of computer-controlled bells that play specially commissioned pieces on a daily basis.

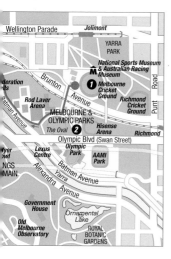

ARTS CENTRE

Follow the river past Federation Square *(see p.42)* and cross to the other bank via Princes Bridge. On the western side of St Kilda Road is one of the city's major visual landmarks, the distinctive latticed spire of the **Arts Centre** ❹ (100 St Kilda Road; tel: 9281 8000; www.the artscentre.com.au). The state's preeminent performing arts complex, it comprises the State Theatre, Hamer Hall, Playhouse Theatre and Fairfax Studio. Designed by architect Roy Grounds, who also designed the nearby NGV International *(see p.66)*, the building hasn't worn too well since opening in 1982, and its interiors were looking particularly dated. Acknowledging this, the Victoria State Government invested in a A$128.5 million redevelopment of Hamer Hall (principal venue for the Melbourne Symphony Orchestra), to offer audiences a better experience.

Performing Arts Collection

The Arts Centre houses the Performing Arts Collection, over 200,000 items relating to the history of performing arts in Australia, including personal memorabilia from artists. A regular exhibition programme showcases items from the collection, many of which have been donated by the artists. Past subjects have included Kylie Minogue, Barry Humphries (aka Dame Edna Everage) and Nick Cave.

Below: Wirth's Circus made way for the Arts Centre and is commemorated in a mosaic.

The Spiegeltent

One of the Arts Centre's most popular attractions is the Spiegeltent, a travelling entertainment salon that makes an appearance in the forecourt every year during the Melbourne International Art Festival *(see p.21)*. Dating from the early 20th century, there are only a handful of these flamboyantly decorated European 'mirror tents' left. During the festival, it hosts cabaret, live music and artists' talks.

SOUTHBANK

Leaving the Arts Centre, walk back towards the river and take any of the connected pathways or stairs down to **Southbank ❺**, a wide paved promenade along the river. There are plenty of tourist cafés and restaurants here including the popular dim sum restaurant **Red Emperor**, see ⑪①. The main attraction, however, is the promenade

itself. After sunset, the view of the city skyline is spiked with the spire of St Paul's Cathedral, the dome of Flinders Street Station and a constellation of glowing office towers. Make sure you check out the sculptures on the Sandridge Bridge as you walk by.

Behind the Southgate development (accessed via Southgate Avenue) is **Eureka Tower ❻**, the tallest building in Melbourne and supposedly the highest residential tower in the world. Vertiginous views can be enjoyed from **Skydeck 88** (Riverside Quay; tel: 96 93 8888; www.eurekalookout.com.au; daily 10am–10pm; charge) on – you guessed it – the building's 88th floor.

CROWN CASINO

Backtrack to Southbank Promenade, continue walking west and cross Queensbridge Street to arrive at **Crown Casino ❼** (tel: 9292 8888; www.crowncasino.com.au; daily 24 hrs). The complex presents a relatively boring face to the water – there's only a modicum of Vegas-style glitz and glamour here – but it has a cinema complex and a smorgasbord of five-star restaurants, including **Rockpool Bar & Grill**, see ⑪②, and **Bistro Guillaume**, see ⑪③.

MELBOURNE AQUARIUM

Opposite the Casino, accessed via Kings Bridge, is the **Melbourne Aquarium ❽** (corner King and Wil-

Art on the Docks
When the Victorian State Government gave the go-ahead for a private-sector redevelopment of Melbourne's Docklands, one of its stipulations was that 1 per cent of the development costs be dedicated to an integrated urban art programme. This led to 29 public artworks being commissioned for the precinct, most of which reflect the themes of water, indigenous history, and the industrial and maritime past. Look out for them on your walk. Pictured right is a mosaic on the Yarra's south bank.

liam streets; tel: 9923 5999; www.mel bourneaquarium.com.au; daily 9.30am–6pm, Jan until 9pm; charge). Luckily, the sea creatures on show aren't forced to swim in the murky Yarra – they occupy specially designed tanks, including a 2.2 million-litre (500,000 gallon) Oceanarium where visitors can dive with sharks.

SOUTH WHARF

Returning to the southern bank of the Yarra, you will see the **Melbourne Exhibition Centre** on the right. It is known to locals as Jeff's Shed after Jeff Kennett, the former premier of Victoria whose government funded its construction.

Behind the shed, in the area known as **South Wharf**, is the **Melbourne Convention Centre** ❾ (www.mcec.com. au). Opened in 2009, it is the only 6 Star Green Star environmentally rated convention centre in the world. Within this vicinity is a retail and dining promenade, office tower, Hilton Melbourne South Wharf and the **Melbourne Maritime Museum** ❿ (tel: 9699 9760; www.polly woodside.com.au; daily 9.30am–5pm; charge), a showcase for the beautifully restored three-masted iron barque *Polly Woodside*, launched in Belfast in 1885.

DOCKLANDS

Continue along the Yarra Promenade and cross the Webb Footbridge across the Yarra to access Melbourne's **Docklands**, subject of a relatively recent mixed-use development. Walk through **Docklands Park**, keeping the huge Etihad Stadium on your right. After 15 minutes or so you will come to **NewQuay**, a mix of residential towers and restaurants overlooking the harbour. **Mecca Bah**, see ⑪④, is the perfect place to stop for an early dinner.

Food and Drink

① RED EMPEROR
Southgate Arts & Leisure Precinct, 3 Southgate Avenue, Southbank; tel: 9699 4170; www.redemperor.au; Mon–Sat noon–3pm, Sun 11am–4pm; $$$
This highly popular Chinese restaurant affords great views of the city and Yarra River. It is known for its excellent service and some of the best dim sum and seafood dishes created by experienced masterchefs.

② ROCKPOOL BAR & GRILL
Crown Casino; tel: 8648 1900; www.rockpool.com.au/ melbourne/rockpool-bar-and-grill; Sun–Fri noon–3pm and 6–11pm, Sat 6–11pm; $$$$
Sydney's Neil Perry caused a few local feathers to fly when he announced his intention to open here in Melbourne, but all was forgiven as soon as his inspired take on comfort cooking was sampled. Make sure your credit card has leverage.

③ BISTRO GUILLAUME
Crown Casino; tel: 9292 4751; www.bistroguillaume. com.au; daily noon–3pm and 6pm–late; $$$
This modern French bistro with stylish surrounds serves classic dishes such as leg of duck confit and steak frites.

④ MECCA BAH
55a NewQuay Promenade, Docklands; tel: 9642 1300; www.meccabah.com; daily 11am–11pm; $
The only eatery of note in the Docklands precinct, stylish Mecca Bah serves fragrant and tasty Middle Eastern and North African dishes that are as pretty as they are light on the wallet. A gem.

KINGS DOMAIN & ROYAL BOTANIC GARDENS

There are two camps in this city: those who define themselves as sophisticated south-of-the-river types and their staunchly north-of-the-river counter-parts. Perhaps the only territory both groups cherish is this green oasis to the immediate east of the city's grand boulevard, St Kilda Road.

DISTANCE 2.75km (1¾ miles)

TIME A half day

START NGV International

END Royal Botanic Gardens

POINTS TO NOTE

To join a tour of Government House, you will need to book at least seven days in advance. To return to the city centre at the end of the walk, catch the no. 8 tram west along Domain Road.

Cause for Tears

In August 1986 Picasso's painting *Weeping Woman* (1937) was stolen from the National Gallery of Victoria by a group calling itself the Australian Cultural Terrorists. The thieves demanded the establishment of a A$25,000 art prize as a ransom, but the gallery refused to meet their demand. Fortunately, an anonymous tip-off led to the undamaged canvas being recovered in a railway station locker two weeks after it first went missing. The culprits have never been identified.

Looking at St Kilda Road today, it is hard to believe that it was once called Baxter's Track, named after a man who used it as a stock route between the southern banks of the Yarra River and the seaside settlement of St Kilda.

After the first bridge over the river was constructed in 1845, approximately 40ha (100 acres) of land to the east of the track was set aside for a botanical reserve (now the Royal Botanic Gardens), and the track itself was upgraded to a tree-lined road. Wealthy colonists purchased land lots along it, built mansions to live in and sent their boys to school at the newly established Church of England Grammar School (now Melbourne Grammar School) half way along its length; they hoped that the presence of the bluestone Victoria Barracks (1856) would protect them from the bushrangers who occasionally held up parties of travellers heading south.

After the construction of Government House in 1876, St Kilda Road's status as the colony's great ceremonial route was confirmed. Today, the road and the Kings Domain and Royal Botanic Gardens on its eastern edge are among the city's most popular tourism and leisure attractions.

NGV INTERNATIONAL

Begin the tour to the south of Federation Square and the Yarra, where **NGV International** ❶ (180 St Kilda Road; tel: 8620 2222; www.ngv.vic.gov.au; Wed–Mon 10am–5pm; permanent collection free, charge for some temporary exhibitions) sits on the corner of St Kilda Road and Southbank Boulevard.

National Gallery of Victoria

Of Melbourne's many cutting-edge cultural institutions, the National Gallery of Victoria (NGV) is the one held most dear by the arts establishment. Established in the 1860s, it remains the pre-eminent art gallery in the country.

Originally housed in the State Library Building in Swanston Street, the NGV's collection was moved here in 1968. The aesthetic merits of Roy Grounds's fortress-like design were hotly debated at that time, but the building has subsequently become one of the most cherished in the state, particularly loved for its sculpture-adorned moat, entrance water wall and Len French-designed Great Hall ceiling. In 2002 the gallery's Australian holdings were moved to Federation Square *(see p.43)*; at the same time the Grounds building was redesigned and enlarged by Italian architect Mario Bellini.

Inside the Gallery

NGV International showcases world-class collections of decorative arts, Asian and Oceanic art, 18th- and 19th-century English painting and European Old Masters. Don't miss Tiepolo's *The Banquet of Cleopatra* (1743–4), Andy Warhol's *Self portrait no.9*, or Picasso's *Weeping Woman* (1937), the subject of a 1986 heist *(see margin, left)*. In conjunction with NGV's 150th anniversary in 2011, the gallery presents new displays to its collection – including art of the Pacific and Japan.

KINGS DOMAIN

Cross St Kilda Road in front of the gallery and walk to **Kings Domain ❷**, a large public park on the southern side of Linlithgow Avenue. Once part of the formal grounds of Government House, the area was redesigned, replanted and opened to the public in 1935 to commemorate Melbourne's centenary.

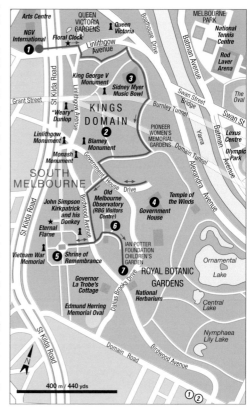

Above from far left: water feature in the Pioneer Women's Memorial Gardens; NGV International.

Outdoor Entertainment

Fancy watching a film under the stars in the Royal Botanic Gardens on a summer night? For details, check www.moon light.com.au. Or perhaps you would prefer to see a play staged on the lawns around the lake? Entertainments including a theatrical performance of *The Wind in the Willows*, based on Kenneth Grahame's much-loved children's book, are often held in the gardens over summer. Check the entertainment listings in the 'EG' section of Friday's *Age* newspaper for details.

Below: details from Kings Domain.

Ahead, on the park's northern edge, is the 1959 **Sidney Myer Music Bowl** ❸. The design for this outdoor music and entertainment venue was inspired by the Hollywood Bowl and is significant for melding revolutionary engineering techniques with an organic structural form that sits perfectly in the landscape of the Domain.

Government House

Head south into the park past the **Pioneer Women's Memorial Gardens**. You will soon see the landmark square tower of **Government House** ❹ (tours Feb–mid-Dec Mon and Wed, book at least seven days in advance; tel: 8663 7260), the home of Victoria's governors since 1876. Modelled on Queen Victoria's Osborne House on the Isle of Wight, this Italianate pile has a huge ballroom that accommodates 2,000 guests and a number of smaller staterooms. Guided tours of the building also take in nearby **La Trobe's Cottage**, a modest prefabricated building that was shipped here from England in 1840 and functioned as the colony's first government house.

The Shrine of Remembrance

Now cross from Government House east to Birdwood Avenue and walk south. Government House may be the largest building in Kings Domain, but it is well and truly overshadowed in the hearts and minds of Melburnians by the **Shrine of Remembrance** ❺ (tel: 9654

8415; www.shrine.org.au; daily 10am–5pm, guided tours 11am and 2pm; free), built to honour the 114,000 Australians who served the British Empire in the Great War and to memorialise the 19,000 who died doing so. A third of Melbourne's population is estimated to have attended the opening ceremony on Armistice Day, 1934.

The shrine's impressive subterranean visitor centre provides educational and exhibition spaces and facilitates entrance into the original building, which has an overly self-important design inspired by the Parthenon at Athens and the Mausoleum at Halicarnassus (one of the seven wonders of the ancient world). Inside, the focal point is a black marble stone of remembrance inscribed 'Greater love hath no man'. On 11 November at 11am, the time when the hostilities of World War I ceased, a ray of light shines through an aperture in the roof and rests on the word 'love'.

The forecourt and its eternal flame were added in 1954 to recognise service in World War II, while the Remembrance Garden commemorates later conflicts. The man and donkey statue in the west forecourt represents John Simpson Kirkpatrick, a stretcher-bearer who rescued wounded men at Gallipoli by carrying them away from the front line on his donkey, almost always braving sniper fire and shrapnel to do so. He was killed at Shrapnel Gully on 19 May 1915, aged only 22.

ROYAL BOTANIC GARDENS

Cross Birdwood Avenue and you will see the **Old Melbourne Observatory** ❻, now the visitor centre for the city's magnificent **Royal Botanic Gardens** (tel: 9252 2300; www.rbg.vic.gov.au; daily Nov–Mar 7.30am–8.30pm, Apr and Sept–Oct 7.30am–6pm, May–Aug 7.30am–5.30pm; free). Land was set aside here for public gardens in 1846, but the design seen now – with sweeping lawns, meandering paths, rocky outcrops and an ornamental lake at its centre – was created between 1879–1909 by the director William Guilfoyle.

The gardens contain a vast range of plants from all over the world, laid out in their respective climatic zones. You can see rainforest giants (on the Australian Rainforest Walk), desert cacti, Alpine wild flowers and temperate shrubs. No one knew how well foreign trees and plants would grow here when planting first began, but the first director, Ferdinand von Mueller, instigated a programme of plant classification, identification and conservation in the gardens' herbarium in 1857, which continues to this day; it is one of the reasons why the botanical gardens are considered among the most important in the world.

Children's Garden

Those travelling with children shouldn't miss the interactive **Ian Potter Foundation Children's Garden** ❼ (Wed–Sun 10am–sunset except for two months in winter, daily during school holidays; free). Here the aim is for kids to learn about nature while having fun – they can pick flowers, get their hands dirty, scramble around in overgrown plant tunnels and find out what's croaking in the pond.

Lunch Options

If you have provisions with you, favourite spots for an alfresco feast are the lake, with its fountain, ducks and swans; and the Temple of the Winds, a classical folly overlooking the Yarra River. Alternatives include the café at the visitor centre or the kiosk near the lake. For a more substantial meal, try **The Botanical**, see ⑪①, or **Bacash**, see ⑪②, in nearby Domain Road.

On Your Bike
Kings Domain and the banks of the Yarra are great bike-riding destinations. Rentabike @ Federation Square (tel: 9654 2762; www.rentabike.net.au; daily 10am–5pm) at Federation Wharf (under Princes Bridge on the Federation Square side of the river) rents out bikes for adults and children by the hour or day.

Food and Drink

① THE BOTANICAL
169 Domain Road; tel: 9820 7888; www.thebotanical.com.au; Mon–Fri 7am–11pm, Sat–Sun 8am–11pm; $$$$
Renowned executive chef Cheong Liew is now helming this well-loved restaurant after a major refurbishment. Located along a leafy street near the Royal Botanic Gardens, this place draws regulars with its plush setting, modern creations and fine wines. There is also a chef's menu with wine matching selection.

② BACASH
175 Domain Road; tel: 9866 3566; www.bacash.com.au; Mon–Fri noon–3pm and 6pm–late, Sat 6pm–late; $$$
This is one of Melbourne's best seafood restaurants, a temple to all things piscatorial. Owner and chef Michael Bacash is serious about his seafood, and lets the quality of his produce speak for itself, eschewing fussy sauces or overly clever combinations.

PRAHRAN, SOUTH YARRA AND TOORAK

These upmarket suburbs on the southern bank of the Yarra are beloved by the local botox and bling brigade. This walk saunters along hip Greville Street, continues down chichi Chapel Street and ventures onto the gilded thoroughfare of Toorak Road, concluding at colonial Como House.

Windsor

Once the province of brickworks, quarries and market gardens, the suburb of Windsor, south of Prahran, may have lost its solid working-class credentials, but it retains a rough-around-the-edges charm beloved by students and arty types. The shops, restaurants and nightclubs at the southern end of Chapel Street are an endearing mix of grunge and glamour – favourites include the Chapel Street Bazaar (nos 217–223), home to vintage furniture, objets d'art and collectors' items; popular nightclub Revolver Upstairs at no. 229 *(see p.123)*; and Middle Eastern restaurant Mama Ganoush at no. 56 *(see p.121)*.

DISTANCE 3.25km (2 miles)
TIME A half day (more if serious shopping is on the agenda)
START Prahran Railway Station
END Como Historic House and Garden
POINTS TO NOTE
The easiest way to get to Prahran Station is to catch the Sandringham Line train from Flinders Street Station. To return to the city centre from Como House, catch the no. 8 tram travelling west along Toorak Road.

The streets of these inner southern suburbs are endowed with dramatically different characters. Chapel Street is bursting at the seams with chichi boutiques and cafés frequented by the cutting-edge crowd, whereas the ritzy retail strip of Toorak Road has an older, moneyed vibe. Greville Street and Commercial Road are different again, one carrying the retail baggage of a hippie past and the other being flam-boyantly gay and lesbian. Visitors come here to shop until they drop, cavort among the café culture and party like crazy – it's a high-velocity village where you will need stamina and a well-charged credit card to fit in.

The Area's Origins

The first subdivision of land in this part of town was in 1840, with large Crown allotments being sold in what was to become the City of Prahran. These were in turn divided into desirable estates on the hills and far less desirable blocks of land in the swampy lower-lying areas. The different land prices inevitably led to the municipality developing two distinct demographics – upper class and working class – as well as a wide array of building styles.

Initially accessed via a punt across the Yarra (hence the name Punt Road for the main traffic artery from the north), Prahran boomed in the 1880s after a cable tram service was introduced in 1888. In 1887 the municipality was divided into four wards: Prahran, South Yarra, Toorak and Windsor.

PRAHRAN

Pronounced 'P'ran', this suburb has as its spine chaotic Chapel Street. Traffic here is always bumper-to-bumper, so the best way to arrive is by train. From **Prahran Railway Station** ❶, walk east into Greville Street. Once a hippie mecca, this strip is now known for its funky clothing boutiques and casual cafés. At the end of the street is the stolid **Prahran Town Hall** ❷, a Victorian Italianate pile dating from 1861.

Prahran Market

From the Town Hall corner, turn left into Chapel Street, walk north to the major cross street of Commercial Road. Located here is the popular **Prahran Market** ❸ (nos 163–165; tel: 8290 8220; www.prahranmarket.com. au; Tue, Thur and Sat dawn–5pm, Fri dawn–6pm, Sun 10am–3pm), dating from 1891. Generally considered the second-best market in the city (after Queen Victoria Market, *see p.39*), it sells top-quality fresh produce and has a western annexe that hosts a food hall and gourmet kitchenware/grocery stores such as **The Essential Ingredient**. Foodies can also check out the cooking school here.

On Tuesday, Thursday and Sunday from 9.30am to 12.30pm, Australian Farmyard Friends gives kids a chance to get up close to farm animals such as lambs, goats and rabbits.

Chapel Street Boutiques

After backtracking to Chapel Street, continue north and you will come to one of Melbourne's best boutique belts, home to Australian fashion labels such as **Bettina Liano**, **Alannah Hill** and **Collette Dinnigan**. Also in this stretch is the **Oriental Tea House**, see ⑪① *(p.73)*, a popular all-day *yum cha* joint.

SOUTH YARRA

Arriving at the major intersection of Chapel Street and Toorak Road, you

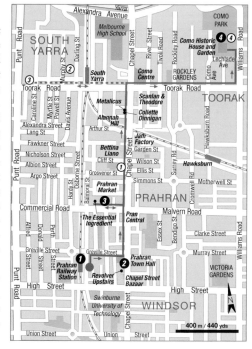

Above from left: necklaces in a Toorak jewellery shop; Como Historic House.

Below: ersatz period street lamps in Toorak.

have two choices. If you are keen to indulge in some more shopping, veer west up the gentle incline to South Yarra Village. The boutiques here sell international designer goods and are guaranteed to give your credit card a serious workout.

If you are after lunch, there is also an impressive array of cafés and restaurants to choose from along this strip, such as **Harveys**, see ⑪②, and **France-Soir**, see ⑪③. Alternatively, you can choose to walk east past the huge Como Centre, a huge office and retail development, to Toorak, Melbourne's equivalent of Beverly Hills or Bel-Air.

TOORAK

Although a close neighbour, staid Toorak is worlds away from sybaritic South Yarra. Home to more than a quorum of Melbourne's establishment, it oozes conservatism, wealth and power. Here, credit cards are platinum, European sedans are a dime a dozen and blonde highlights are mandatory.

A walk around the streets showcases myriad mansions dating from the late 19th and 20th centuries, but all pale into insignificance when compared with the magnificent National Trust-run property Como House, accessed by heading east on Toorak Road and, after about seven blocks, turning left into Williams Road and walking one block north.

Como House

Como Historic House and Garden ❹ (corner of Williams Road and Lechlade Avenue; tel: 9827 2500; www.comohouse.com.au; daily 10am–4pm; charge) started life in 1847 as a single-storey villa constructed from bricks made using Yarra River mud. Nestled amid 20ha (50 acres) of bushland, it was a one-hour journey by horse, carriage and punt to and from the city,

where the original owner, Edward Eyre Williams, worked as a barrister. Sold to a Scotsman, John Brown, in 1853, the original building was soon adorned with a second storey, extensive outbuildings and a formal garden designed by William Sangster, one of the colony's best-known gardeners. This orgy of expenditure was to have an unfortunate outcome, with Brown suffering financial reverses and being forced to sell the property in 1864.

The new owners were Charles and Caroline Armytage, wealthy pastoralists from the Western District, who used Como as their Melbourne base. Renowned for their entertaining, they added a ballroom and billiard room, where the cream of colonial society socialised, and furnished the house with furniture and objets d'art purchased from Europe, leaving an indelible impression.

After George and Caroline died, the house was inherited by their three unmarried daughters, who subdivided the land in 1911 and 1921, and then sold the house, furnishings and garden to the National Trust in 1959.

Enthusiastic and knowledgeable volunteer guides take visitors on a guided tour of the house and outbuildings, but the 2ha (5-acre) garden can be explored unaccompanied. The sweeping views down to the Yarra are impressive, and the vegetable garden, sloping lawns, flower walks and water features are quite lovely.

After you have admired everything, do as the colonial gentry did and indulge in the ritual of afternoon tea at the charming **Café Bursaria**, see ⑪④, in the estate's grounds.

Food and Drink

① ORIENTAL TEA HOUSE

455 Chapel Street, South Yarra; tel: 9826 0168; www.orientalteahouse.com.au; Sun–Wed 10am–10pm, Thur 10am–11pm, Fri–Sat 10am–11.30pm; $

Giving a South Yarra twist to the traditional Chinese tea house, this stylish emporium tempts with fragrant teas and tasty *yum cha* morsels, sells tea and accessories from its retail section and even offers consultations with a doctor trained in traditional Chinese medicine.

② HARVEYS

10 Murphy Street, South Yarra; tel: 9867 3605; www.harveysrestaurant.com.au; daily 8am–2pm, Tue–Sat 6–10pm; $$$

Renowned for its breakfasts (with or without a glass of imported bubbly), this stylish eatery would be equally at home in Bel-Air as it is here in South Yarra. The food is consistently delicious and the scene on the terrace showcases the artful air-kissing techniques of an army of regulars.

③ FRANCE-SOIR

11 Toorak Road, South Yarra; tel: 9866 8569; www.france-soir.com.au; daily noon–3pm and 6pm–midnight; $$$

For classic French dishes served with a soupçon of sophistication and buckets of bonhomie you need go no further than this Melbourne institution. The steak béarnaise is a perennial favourite, as is the *magret de canard* (whole duck breast) and steak tartare.

④ CAFÉ BURSARIA

Como Historic House and Garden, South Yarra; tel: 9824 2889; winter months Wed–Sun 10am–4pm; $

One of the best cafés in South Yarra is tucked away in the outbuildings of historic Como House. It is rare to be served a perfectly brewed cup of tea or a light-as-a-feather scone, but that is what is on offer here. The light lunches tempt every palate and the weekend brunches are renowned.

SOUTH MELBOURNE AND ALBERT PARK

Residents of this upmarket enclave rarely stray too far from home, content to reside in its grand Victorian mansions, socialise in its chic cafés and work out at its impressive sporting facilities. Having tasted their privileged lifestyles, conclude culturally at the Australian Centre for Contemporary Art.

Below: Clarendon Street façade and signpost.

DISTANCE 7.25km (4½ miles)
TIME A full day
START South Melbourne Market
END Australian Centre for Contemporary Art
POINTS TO NOTE
To reach the starting point for this walk, catch the no. 96 tram from Bourke Street in the city centre and get off at South Melbourne station (stop no. 127). To return to the city at the end of the walk, catch tram no. 1 from outside the Australian Centre of Contemporary Art on Sturt Street (stop no. 18).

Food and Drink
① GAS
253 Coventry Street, South Melbourne; tel: 9690 0217; Mon–Fri 8am–6pm, Sat–Sun 8am–5pm; $
Ladies who lunch share tables with ad execs and market traders at this exemplar of South Melbourne's chic café culture. Regulars swear by the tasty Middle Eastern and Mediterranean dishes including lamb kofta and Spanish omelettes with chorizo and goat's cheese.

Strategically located between Port Phillip Bay and the city centre, these inner southern suburbs are the favoured stamping grounds of Melbourne's advertising and media professionals and have a sophisticated sheen to prove it.

It's a far cry from the district's humble beginnings, when canvas tents were erected on the southern side of the Yarra River to house temporarily the overflow of immigrants landing in the colony en route to the fabled goldfields of central Victoria. Originally known as Emerald Hill, South Melbourne became an independent municipality in 1855 and soon outgrew its boundaries, extending into the surrounding districts of Port Melbourne, Albert Park and Middle Park.

From 1890 cable trams rattled up and down the thriving commercial hub of Clarendon Street, linking the city centre with the desirable residential pocket of Albert Park and the popular sea baths at Kerferd Road Beach. Physically, not much has changed here since that period.

SOUTH MELBOURNE

Alight from the tram from the city centre and, immediately ahead, you will see **South Melbourne Market** ❶ (corner Coventry and Cecil streets; tel: 9209 6295; www.southmelbourne market.com.au; Wed and Sat–Sun 8am–4pm, Fri 8am–5pm). Locals have been shopping here since 1867, and the jumble of produce stands, food stalls and hawkers is endearingly eclectic, selling everything from sausages to saucepans.

The surrounding streets are home to a cluster of cafés specialising in brunch – to get into the local swing of things walk east along Coventry Street, claim a seat at **GAS**, see ⑪①, and soak up its laidback latte-driven ambience.

Clarendon Street Precinct

Keep walking along Coventry Street and you will soon reach a wide boule-vard lined with Victorian-era buildings. Every Melbourne suburb has its equiva-lent of an English high street, and here in South Melbourne Clarendon Street has always claimed this honour. Its shopping options are nothing to get excited about (try Coventry Street instead), but its historic shopfronts com-plete with iron verandas attest to the suburb's long mercantile history.

South Melbourne Town Hall

Turn right and walk two blocks until you reach Bank Street; the **South Melbourne Town Hall** ❷ is on the crest of a small hill to the west. Built in 1879–80 on the highest point in the suburb (the 'Emerald Hill' that gave the suburb its original name), this

Above: jogging by Albert Park Lake.

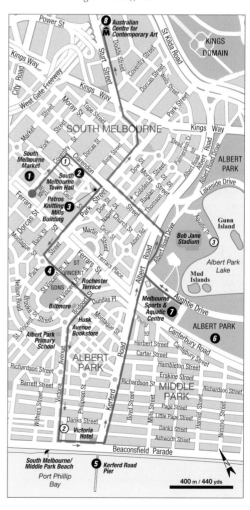

Coffee House Craze
In the late 19th century approximately 60 grand coffee palaces were built around Melbourne by the temperance movement to provide alcohol-free alternatives to the city's numerous rowdy public houses. The Albert Park Coffee Palace, built in 1887–9 at 152 Bridport Street, was one of these. Converted into a private hotel and renamed the Biltmore in 1928, it was turned into residential apartments in the 1990s.

Below: market sign.

handsome building in the classical style has an imposing clock tower and giant Corinthian-order portico.

Back on Clarendon Street, continue walking until you reach the next intersection, Park Street. Cross the street and look back towards the city to admire the façade of the **Patros Knitting Mills Building ❸** on the northern side of the street at nos 256–264. This two-storey terrace, featuring Gothic-style windows and a square tower, was built in the 1880s to contain shops and residences, and continues to do so today.

ALBERT PARK

Walk west along Park Street, cross Ferrars Street, follow the tram tracks and turn south into Montague Street. You will find yourself in the middle of one of Melbourne's most prestigious residential precincts, **St Vincent Place ❹**. Designed in 1854–5 to resemble square developments in London, it is dominated by its central gardens and huge buildings such as **Rochester Terrace** at nos 33–51, dating from 1879.

Albert Park Village
Continue walking south to come to Bridport Street, the heart of Albert Park Village. The scene here is mon-eyed professional, with statement sunglasses and mandatory smart-casual outfits in neutral colours. Weekend brunch is an air-kissing free-for-all, but the weekday lunch scene is more sedate. Admire the designer frocks and accessories in **Husk** at no. 123 Dundas Place or browse in the excellent **Avenue Bookstore** at no. 127. Of the many handsome buildings in this precinct, the four-storeyed **Biltmore** (at no. 152) is the most imposing *(see margin, left)*.

South Melbourne Beach
Follow the tram line and, at 2–36 Victoria Avenue, you will pass the heritage-listed **Albert Park Primary School**, which dates from 1874. At the end of the street is a modest strip of sand known as **South Melbourne/Middle Park Beach**. Look right and in the distance you will see Station Pier, the terminal for cruise ships, aircraft carriers and the huge car ferries that ply the waters of Bass Strait between Melbourne and Launceston in Tasmania.

Turn left and walk along Beaconsfield Parade until you come to the **Kerferd Road Pier** ❺, built in 1887–9. In the late 19th century Melburnians flocked to this area at weekends to spend time at the swimming baths (since demolished), promenade on the pier and enjoy a meal or a drink at Hotel Victoria at the corner of Kerferd Road and Beaconsfield Parade. Today, this heritage building houses **The Victorian**, a restaurant that offers a modern Australian menu with Middle Eastern and Mediterranean influences. Meanwhile, **Stavros**, see ⑪②, not far from Beaconsfield Parade also serves excellent Greek food and wines.

Albert Park and Lake

Turn left into Kerferd Road and walk until you reach **Albert Park** ❻, a huge recreational reserve set around a lake where Melburnians walk, jog, birdwatch, picnic, sail and practise their golf drive. It is also home to the Australian Formula One Grand Prix held in March each year *(see p.22)*.

The park's most popular attraction is the **Melbourne Sports & Aquatic Centre** ❼ (MSAC; Aughtie Drive; tel: 9926 1555; www.msac.com.au; Mon–Fri 5.30am–10pm, Sat–Sun 7am–8pm; charge), which has Olympic-sized indoor and outdoor swimming pools, plus a wave pool, sauna, spa and steam room. Overlooking the lake is **The Point**, see ⑪③, a highly regarded steak restaurant where you can enjoy lunch.

AUSTRALIAN CENTRE FOR CONTEMPORARY ART

Leave the reserve at the Albert Road exit and walk down Clarendon Street until you reach Park Street. From this corner, catch the no. 1 tram heading towards East Coburg and alight at stop no. 18 in front of the huge rusted-steel monolith that houses the **Australian Centre for Contemporary Art** ❽ (ACCA; 111 Sturt Street; tel: 9697 9999; www.accaonline.org.au; Tue–Fri 10am–5pm, Sat–Sun 11am–6pm; free). This visually arresting building was designed by multi-award-winning local architects Wood Marsh, who were briefed to design a sculpture in which to show art. Five exhibitions annually showcase Australian and international contemporary art.

Food and Drink

② STAVROS
183 Victoria Avenue, Albert Park; tel: 9699 5618; www.stavrostavern.com.au; Tue–Sun 6–10pm; $
This popular Greek tavern has been around since 1979. Dig into hearty moussaka and char-grilled octopus, complemented by fine wines. On Fridays and Saturdays, enjoy live Greek music alongside some dancing and plate smashing.

③ THE POINT
Aquatic Drive, Albert Park Lake; tel: 9682 5566; www.the pointalbertpark.com.au; daily noon–3pm and 6pm–late; $$$
As a nation, Australia has more than its fair share of cattle stations. Strange, then, that good steakhouses are few and far between. This sophisticated example is located on the shore of Albert Park Lake and is consistently commended for the quality and cooking of its beef. Fish dishes feature too.

ST KILDA
AND BALACLAVA

Although geographically close, these two suburbs are poles apart in every other respect. St Kilda has a sybaritic seaside-resort ambience first acquired in the 1850s, while sensible Balaclava is home to a large chunk of the city's Orthodox Jewish population and has always had a stolidly suburban air.

St Kilda's Troubadour

St Kilda has always had a vibrant live-music scene and many local musicians have sung tributes to its charms. The best-known of these is perhaps singer-songwriter Paul Kelly, whose song *From St Kilda to King's Cross* includes the lyrics 'I want to see the sun go down from St Kilda Esplanade/ Where the beach needs reconstruction, where the palm trees have it hard.'

DISTANCE 4.25km (2¾ miles)
TIME A full day
START Jewish Museum of Australia
END Balaclava Railway Station
POINTS TO NOTE
To reach the Jewish Museum of Australia from the city centre, catch tram no. 67 or no. 3 from Swanston Street and get off at stop no. 32; the museum is a two-minute walk to the east.

To return to the city, catch a train from Balaclava Station to Flinders Street Station or hop on tram no. 16 or no. 3 to Melbourne University via Swanston Street.

To visit Rippon Lea in Elsternwick, catch the Sandringham line train from Balaclava Station one stop to Rippon Lea Station. Alternatively, catch tram no. 67 to Carnegie from Balaclava Station and alight at stop no. 42. To return to the city, catch the train to Flinders Street or the tram to Swanston Street.

St Kilda

The bayside suburb of St Kilda has always been Melbourne's favourite playground. A train line from the city centre to the bay was built as early as 1857, and many of the colony's earliest entrepreneurs and professionals followed it, building mansions on St Kilda Hill where they could escape the smells, noise and occasional pestilence of the city centre.

When cable trams reached the suburb in 1888, less affluent Melburnians flocked here at weekends and holidays to enjoy a dip in the sea baths, a promenade along the pier or a stroll around the pleasure gardens. The more sedentary among them opted to watch the moving pictures at the Palais, enjoy a mild flirtation at the Palais de Danse or ride the carousel at Luna Park. Many day-trippers enjoyed their weekends here so much that they chose to move into one of the profusion of boarding houses that operated from 1890, or rent an apartment in one of the modern blocks constructed in the first decades of the 20th century.

The existence of these apartment blocks means that the suburb has long been the most densely built and populated area of Melbourne. Today, it is home to young professionals and arty types, with blow-ins from every corner of the city descending on Fitzroy and Acland streets at weekends to enjoy its cafés, bars, restaurants and slightly seedy nocturnal street life.

Balaclava

In contrast, Balaclava has retained the amenities and atmosphere of a staid and predominantly Jewish suburb, with kosher butchers, haberdashers and bagel shops managing to hold their own against a creeping influx of trendy cafés, wine bars and boutiques.

JEWISH MUSEUM OF AUSTRALIA

Start at the **Jewish Museum of Australia** ❶ (26 Alma Road; tel: 8534 3600; www.jewishmuseum.com.au; Tue–Thur 10am–4pm, Sun 10am–5pm; charge). The multimedia exhibits at this community museum give visitors a crash course in Jewish history and culture, as well as documenting the history of Jews in Australia.

Visitors can also take a guided tour of the nearby 1,000-seat **St Kilda Hebrew Congregation Synagogue** at 10–12 Charnwood Grove (tours Tue–Thur 12.30pm, Sun 12.30pm and 3pm); it was built in 1927 on the site of a previous synagogue dating from 1872.

Above from far left: jogging along St Kilda beach; suburb insignia; café in Acland Street; menorah in the Jewish Museum.

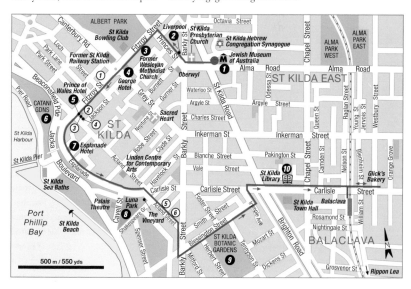

ST KILDA HILL

Leaving the museum, turn right, cross the busy highway and walk along Princes Street. On the next corner is the bluestone **St Kilda Presbyterian Church**, with its distinctive witch-hat tower. Directly opposite the church, on the northwestern corner is **Liverpool ②**, a mansion built in 1888 by Nathaniel Levi (1830–1908), the first Jewish member of the Parliament of Victoria.

In this immediate area, which is known as St Kilda Hill, you will notice other historically significant mansions, including **Oberwyl** on the corner of Princes and Burnett streets. This Regency-style mansion has functioned as a private residence, exclusive girls' school and the headquarters of the Victorian Alliance Française. Continuing west down Princes Street, you will soon come to the suburb's most famous strip.

FITZROY STREET

Turning left into Fitzroy Street, you will soon pass a pretty bluestone church building covered in creeping vine. This is the **Former Wesleyan Methodist Church ③**, built in 1857–8 to host services for the prosperous colonists who resided in St Kilda in its early days. On the other side of the street, a bit further on is the **St Kilda Bowling Club**, a local institution. Hosting games of bowls, quoits, croquet and skittles, the clubhouse was established on this site in 1865, and the present building dates from 1926. Next door is the **Former St Kilda Railway Station**, a rare example of an intact Victorian-era railway

Food and Drink

① MIRKA AT TOLARNO HOTEL
42 Fitzroy Street, St Kilda; www.mirkatolarnohotel.com; tel: 9525 3088; daily noon–late; $$$
French-born artist Mirka Mora and her art-dealer husband Georges ran a legendary bohemian restaurant here in the 1960s, and Mirka's charming murals have survived a recent, very classy, renovation. The menu created by renowned chef Guy Grossi features perfectly executed French and Italian dishes.

② CAFÉ DI STASIO
31 Fitzroy Street, St Kilda; tel: 9525 3999; daily noon–3pm and 6–11pm; $$$
Restaurateur Ronnie Di Stasio has endowed his self-named restaurant with a unique sense of theatricality as well as a faithful adherence to unfussy Italian cuisine. The wine list is just as impressive (Di Stasio has his own vineyard in the Yarra Valley). The well-priced set-lunch menu of two courses and a glass of wine is a Melbourne institution. Book ahead.

③ IL FORNAIO
2 Acland Street, St Kilda; tel: 9534 2922; www.ilfornaio. net.au; daily Mon–Fri 7am–5pm, Sat–Sun 8am–5pm; $
The industrial-chic decor may scream 21st-century St Kilda, but the delectable breads, pastries and cakes served at this bakery-café are classically European. It claims to serve Melbourne's best lattes.

④ LAU'S FAMILY KITCHEN
4 Acland Street, St Kilda; tel: 8598 9880; Sun–Fri noon–3pm, 6–10pm, Sat 6–10pm; $$
Forget chandeliers, tuxedoed waiters or huge numbered menus – what's on show here is freshly prepared and consummately presented Cantonese cuisine served in fashionably minimal surroundings.

station. Trains no longer run to St Kilda, and the station now functions as a tram stop and restaurant cluster, including **Pizza e Birra** *(see p.121)*.

Lunch Options

Opposite the station is the huge **George Hotel** ❹, a grand resort-style hotel dating from 1857. In the late 20th century it became famous as a live-music venue of unparalleled grunginess (this is one of the places where Nick Cave and the first incarnation of the Bad Seeds started their careers), and it now houses fashionable apartments.

Although Fitzroy Street is full of restaurants and cafés, not too many are worthy of recommendation. Exceptions include **Mirka at Tolarno Hotel**, see ⑪①, and **Café Di Stasio**, see ⑪②.

On the corner of Acland Street is one of the suburb's best-known buildings, the **Prince of Wales Hotel** ❺. Once infamous for its rough-as-guts front bar, it was extensively renovated in the 1990s, and is now home to a boutique hotel *(see p.115)*, restaurant and spa retreat. If you turn left off Fitzroy Street at the Prince corner, you will encounter a raft of popular eateries including **Il Fornaio**, see ⑪③, and **Lau's Family Kitchen**, see ⑪④.

Catani Gardens

At the western end of the street are the historic **Catani Gardens** ❻, a 6ha (15-acre) reserve on the foreshore of St Kilda Beach. The landscaping and plantings here date from the late 1920s, and the most distinctive feature is the many tapering palm trees lining the paths.

Above from far left: tram to St Kilda; at the Bowling Club.

Below: the Prince of Wales is now a boutique hotel.

Modern Evil

For much of the 20th century, St Kilda had an unsavoury reputation as the home of crime, prostitution and drugs. This peaked in the 1940s, when American and Australian servicemen on leave flocked here to solicit the favours of local girls, some of whom were ladies of the night. From 1943–7, local artist Albert Tucker documented this era in his acclaimed series of paintings, *Images of Modern Evil*.

UPPER ESPLANADE

Continue walking along Fitzroy Street and follow the tram line along the Upper Esplanade, best known for the **Esplanade Hotel** ❼ (aka the 'Espy'), an endearingly egalitarian watering hole and live-music venue. Apartments in the 1930s blocks along this stretch of the Upper Esplanade are hotly sought after but rarely available; sunset views over the bay and blissfully briny breezes mean that they are considered blue-chip real estate.

LUNA PARK

As you walk towards the end of the Esplanade you will spot the twin cupolas of the **Palais Theatre**, a former picture palace dating from 1927. You

Right: St Kilda Botanic Gardens.

may also hear shrill screams issuing from its neighbour, **Luna Park** ❽ (18 Lower Esplanade; tel: 9525 5033; www.lunapark.com.au; hours vary, check website; free entry, ride ticket charge), built in 1912 and long famous as the home of the exhilarating Scenic Railway rollercoaster. Consider taking a spin on the funpark's gorgeous carousel (with 68 hand painted horses), which was built in America in 1913 and installed here in 1923.

ACLAND STREET

At the roundabout, enter the tree-lined shopping strip of Acland Street, known for its block of shops selling decadent European-style cakes. This is a good spot for a break – you can scoff a cake and coffee at **Monarch Cake Shop**, see 🍴⑤, enjoy a leisurely lunch with the locals at ever-popular **Cicciolina**, see 🍴⑥, or sink a beer or two at **The Vineyard**, an unpretentious bar with outdoor seating where backpackers, bohemians and the occasional besuited businessman rub shoulders.

ST KILDA BOTANIC GARDENS

Walk to the end of Acland Street, veer right into Barkly Street and then turn off to the left at Blessington Street. Here you will find the **St Kilda Botanic Gardens** ❾ (corner Blessington and Tennyson streets; www.port

phillip.vic.gov.au/st_kilda_botanic.htm; daily sunrise–sunset; free), established in 1861. There's a subtropical rainforest conservatory to marvel at, plus a giant chessboard and an ornamental pond. The gardens are particularly wonderful between November and April, when the Alistair Clark Memorial Rose Garden is in full bloom.

CARLISLE STREET

Leave the gardens and continue walking east along Blessington Street. Cross the manic intersection of St Kilda Road/Brighton Road and enter Carlisle Street, home to the **St Kilda Town Hall**. Look out for the **St Kilda Library** ⑩ on the left-hand side of street. Local architectural firm Ashton Raggatt McDougall was commissioned to renovate the library in the 1990s, and added a witty façade resembling a giant book. The building visually complements the same firm's extensions to the Town Hall.

The shopping strip to the east of the library and Town Hall is notable for being the favoured patch of Melbourne's Jewish community, and is home to bagel shops, kosher butchers and stores specialising in accoutrements such as menorahs. The most popular store here is **Glick's Bakery** at no. 330; it sells boiled bagels, cinnamon rolls and other tasty treats.

From Glick's Bakery, backtrack two streets to **Balaclava Railway Station**, from where you can catch a train back to the city or continue on to the National Trust property Rippon Lea *(see feature, below)*.

Above from far left: Palais Theatre; Luna Park entrance; at a cake shop on Acland Street.

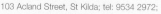

Food and Drink

⑤ **MONARCH CAKE SHOP**

103 Acland Street, St Kilda; tel: 9534 2972; www.monarchcakes.com.au; daily 7.30am–9pm; $

This outlet was established by a Polish émigré in 1934 and eventually bought by current owner Gideon Markham in 1996. The best-seller here is the rich chocolate *kooglhoupf*, a large ring-shaped cake made according to the shop's original recipe. Grab a table by the side-walk and tuck into some good old-fashioned cakes with coffee.

⑥ **CICCIOLINA**

130 Acland Street, St Kilda; tel: 9525 3333; www.cicciolina stkilda.com.au; Mon–Sat noon–11pm, Sun noon–10pm; $$

How do we love thee, Cicciolina? Let us count the ways. We love your modern seasonal menu, your reasonable prices and your welcoming rear bar. But, most of all, we love your boisterous atmosphere. Ours is a true passion put to use.

Rippon Lea

Built by Frederick Sargood, a businessman and politician who made his fortune selling soft goods on the Victorian goldfields, the Romanesque-style Rippon Lea (192 Hotham Street, Elsternwick; tel: 9523 6095; www. ripponleaestate.com.au; Sept–Apr daily 10am–5pm, May–Aug Thur–Sun 10am–4pm; charge) is one of the few remaining great 19th-century suburban estates in Melbourne. Building commenced in 1868 and continued until 1897, with an Art Deco ballroom and swimming pool added by subsequent owners in 1939. The wonderful garden features a lake, waterfalls, mature trees, fernery, a hill and grotto, all of which were designed or planted between 1868 and the 1880s.

WILLIAMSTOWN

Melburnians flock to the quaint waterside suburb of Williamstown to enjoy weekend promenades along Nelson Place and admire the city skyline across the bay. This relaxed walk showcases the suburb's village atmosphere, maritime heritage and historic streetscapes.

Scienceworks

Both ferry companies will stop on request at Scienceworks (2 Booker Street, Spotswood; tel: 131 102; www.museum victoria.com.au/scienceworks; daily 10am–4.30pm; charge), an interactive museum that aims to make science an adventure for the visitor. The museum incorporates the old Spotswood Pumping Station, home to huge engines that once pumped the sewage and associated odours from 'Marvellous Smellbourne' as it was once facetiously called, as well as a state-of-the-art planetarium (one show daily on week-days, one show hourly at weekends).

DISTANCE Walk: 5km (3¼ miles)

TIME A half day (or a full day if you visit Scienceworks as well)

START Gem Pier

END Williamstown Beach

POINTS TO NOTE

Melbourne River Cruises (tel: 8610 2600; www.melbcruises.com.au) depart from Berth 5, Lower Promenade, Southgate, between 10.30am and 2.30pm (May–Sept) or 3.30pm (Oct–Apr) every day (taking about an hour). The number of sailings increases in summer and at weekends. The last return service leaves Williamstown at 3.30pm (May–Sept) or 4.30pm (Oct–Apr). Williamstown Ferries (aka Bay and River Cruises; tel: 9517 9444; www.williamstownferries.com.au) runs from Berth 1 daily between 10.30am and 4.30pm. The last return sailing from Gem Pier is at 5.30pm.

You can also go by train from Southern Cross or Flinders Street railway stations.

Much of Williamstown's rich maritime history remains, giving the suburb a historical resonance appreciated by salty seadogs and landlubbers alike.

History of Williamstown

The first settlers of what would become the colony of Victoria arrived by sailing ship in 1835 from Van Diemen's Land, alighting at Point Gellibrand with 500 sheep and 500 cattle. In 1837 the new-born settlement was divided into two towns: Melbourne, named after the prime minister of the time, Lord Melbourne, and Williamstown, which bore the name of King William IV.

The deep harbour at Point Gellibrand was chose for the colony's main port, and a lighthouse and landing pier were built there. The huge Alfred Graving Dock, home to a colonial navy that was to be the forerunner of the Royal Australian Navy, followed in 1874.

In 1887 engineers finished work on the Coode Canal. By cutting out a long, looping bend in the Yarra where the river wound through the West Melbourne swamp, the canal brought ships right into the heart of Melbourne, bypassing Williamstown.

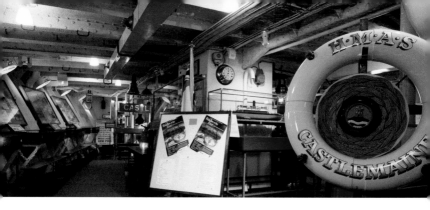

Gradually the once-important port was relegated to the status of a backwater. Fortunately, its grand 19th-century commercial buildings, residences and boat-building industries were retained and today endow the suburb with an endearing time-capsule feel.

GEM PIER

The most enjoyable way to get to Williamstown is to take a ferry from Southgate just across the Yarra from Flinders Street Station. If you are interested in hands-on science, ask to stop en route at **Scienceworks** *(see margin, left)*.

Alight at **Gem Pier ❶**. Williamstown's first jetty was built here between 1839–47, and the pier has subsequently been demolished and rebuilt three times – the last being in 1992.

HMAS *Castlemaine*

Locally built **HMAS *Castlemaine*** (www.hmascastlemaine.org.au; Sat–Sun 10am–4pm; charge), a 1941 minesweeper that saw active service in New Guinea and Northern Australia during World War II, is moored here and is a big hit with kids, who love clambering aboard and seeing the wheel, compasses and radar screen at the helm.

Above from far left: yachts moored in front of apartments in Williamstown; inside HMAS *Castlemaine*.

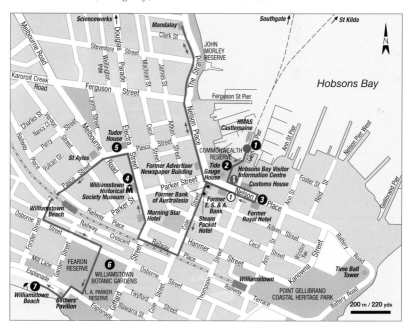

COMMONWEALTH RESERVE

Walk from the pier towards the park ahead, known as the **Commonwealth Reserve ②**. Early immigrants were carried from their sailing ships on the shoulders of burly seamen and dumped onto unprepossessing mudflats lined with saltbush and a scattering of modest buildings. The mudflats were replaced between 1880–1930 by this harbourside park, created using earth dredged from shipping channels.

In the reserve you will find a **Tide Gauge House**, which once protected a valuable tide gauge imported from England; the 1857 structure was moved to its present location from Port Gellibrand in 1955, when the boat harbour was filled in.

Also here is the helpful **Hobsons Bay Visitor Information Centre** (tel: 9932 4310; www.visithobsonsbay.com. au; daily 9am–5pm), which provides clean toilets and free brochures, maps and information about Williamstown.

Craft Market

The popular Williamstown Craft Market (tel: 0402 811 756; www.williamstown craftmarket.com.au) is held in Commonwealth Reserve on the third Sunday of each month from 10am–4pm.

Food and Drink 🍴

① WILLIAMSTOWN MUSSELS FISH AND CHIPPERY

129 Nelson Place; tel: 9399 9961; winter Mon 11.30am–7.30pm, Wed–Sun 11.30am–9pm, summer Sun–Mon, Wed–Thur 11.30am–9pm, Fri–Sat 11.30am–late; $

Forget the overpriced and underwhelming fare on offer in the eateries along Nelson Place. Instead, order fish and chips from this popular takeaway outlet, colonise a bench in Commonwealth Reserve and dine alfresco.

NELSON PLACE

When the gold rush began in the 1850s thousands of diggers were drawn to Victoria. Ships crammed into Hobsons Bay, a new pier was built, and service industries, including shipwrights, banks, boarding houses and pubs, sprang up along the harbour in **Nelson Place ③**. These included the handsome **Customs House**, built in 1873–5 at the approach to Gem Pier; the **Former Royal Hotel** at no. 85, built in 1890 on the site of a previous hotel dating from 1852; the Gothic-style **Former E. S. & A. Bank** at no. 139, built in 1873; the **Former *Advertiser* Newspaper Building** at nos 205–206, built between 1885–8 as the home of the *Williamstown Advertiser* (still published weekly); and the **Former Bank of Australasia** on the corner of Cole Street, which dates from 1876.

The Strand

Those residents made wealthy by these local industries built impressive residences along the western extension of Nelson Place, which was given the genteel name of **The Strand**. Look out for **Mandalay** at no. 24, a colonial Georgian residence built in 1858 for a ship chandler named Captain William Probert.

Fish and Chips

The cafés, restaurants and pubs along Nelson Place are notable for their historic premises rather than their

produce – if you are peckish, the best option is to make your way back towards Gem Pier and order some fish and chips from **Williamstown Mussels Fish and Chippery**, see ⑪①.

HISTORIC PUBS AND HOUSES

From Nelson Place, turn south into Cole Street. On the first corner, at nos 11–13, you will see the **Steam Packet Hotel**, built in 1863 to replace an earlier inn. Continue south and turn right into Railway Place. You will soon come to another historic pub, the 1889 **Morning Star Hotel** at 3 Electra Street.

Williamstown Historical Society Museum

Just up from here at no. 5 is the **Williamstown Historical Society Museum** ❹ (tel: 9397 5423; www.williamstownhistsoc.org.au; Sun 2–5pm or by appointment; free), housed in a Mechanics' Institute building dating from 1860. The museum details the suburb's maritime history and houses other exhibits illustrating life in Williamstown from the 1840s.

At the corner of Electra and Pasco streets is **Tudor House** ❺, built in 1884 for prominent politician and lawyer William Henry Roberts. Its elegant, relatively restrained design stands in contrast to other more ostentatious residences built for public figures during the so-called 'Boom period'. Turn left into Pasco Street to see handsome **St Ayles** at no. 72, which dates from 1891.

Keep on walking and you will reach the **Williamstown Beach Railway Station**, a stop on the oldest government railway line in Victoria. Operating from 1857, it carried steam trains from Spencer Street in central Melbourne to a station at Williamstown Pier (now decommissioned), stopping at North Williamstown, Williamstown Beach and Williamstown stations en route.

BOTANIC GARDENS AND BEACH

Walk under the railway line and turn left into Osborne Street until you reach the **Williamstown Botanic Gardens** ❻, a 4ha (10-acre) reserve established in 1860 and remodelled in 1905. Saunter past the rows of tall palm trees standing sentinel and then through the pine-treed L. A. Parker Reserve, from where you can admire the striking 1930s **Bathers' Pavilion**, now a café and kiosk, on **Williamstown Beach** ❼. This is the most attractive (and probably the cleanest) of Melbourne's suburban beaches.

To return to the city, head back across town to Gem Pier to take the ferry back; alternatively, catch a train from the Williamstown Beach Railway Station.

Above from far left: Nelson Place; perfect seaside lunch fare; Williamstown sunset.

Incredible Hulks
Unlike many of the Australian colonies, Victoria was founded by free settlers rather than convicts. It did, however, have an imported convict population. In the 1850s five rotting prison hulks were moored off Point Gellibrand to house these miscreants. The people incarcerated in these filthy, disease-ridden hulks were put to work mining bluestone from a nearby quarry, which was used to construct many of the suburb's first buildings.

YARRA VALLEY

This postcard-pretty region on Melbourne's eastern edge is perfect for a day trip. At weekends there are nearly as many cars here as there are cows, with Melburnians descending en masse to soak up the valley's views and vintages.

Tourist Information
The helpful Yarra Valley Visitor Information Centre (The Old Courthouse, Harker Street; tel: 5962 2600; www.visit yarravalley.com.au; daily 9am–5pm) in Healesville can book accommodation, supply free maps and tourist brochures, and recommend activities.

Destructive Fires
In 2009 bushfires raged through the Yarra Valley destroying the towns of Marysville and nearby Kinglake. Renowned vineyards, including St Huberts, Domaine Chandon and Yering Station, lost some vines but retained their buildings.

DISTANCE approximately 50km (31 miles) from central Melbourne to Yering Station, plus 34km (21 miles) for this tour and approximately 55km (34 miles) back to Melbourne
TIME A full day
START Yering Station
END Domaine Chandon
POINTS TO NOTE
You will need to rent a car for this excursion *(see p.109)*. From central Melbourne, take the Eastern Freeway and EastLink toll road and exit onto the Maroondah Highway. Continue on the highway through Ringwood and Lilydale until you reach Coldstream. Here, take the left-hand exit to the Melba Highway – Yering Station is 8km (5 miles) away, on the right-hand side of the road. Be sure to organise prepayment of an EastLink trip pass; to do so contact your car-rental company or call 13 54 65.

If you wish to eat at Bella Vedere or Giant Steps/Innocent Bystander Winery it is wise to book ahead, particularly at weekends.

In 1844 surveyor Robert Hoddle followed the course of the Yarra River from Melbourne, travelling through a verdant valley to the east of the town and identifying the river's source in a forest on the slopes of Mount Baw Baw. In doing so, he became one of the first Europeans to discover this particularly picturesque pocket of Victoria.

When gold was discovered here in 1851, the indigenous Wurundjeri people were swiftly displaced by miners, and in the 1880s orchards and dairy farms followed, laying the foundations for the notable wineries and cheese producers now based in the Yarra Valley.

YERING STATION

The Scottish-born Ryrie brothers discovered the joys of the Yarra Valley even earlier than Robert Hoddle, taking up a grazing licence here in 1838. They kept the Wurundjeri name for their land and planted vine cuttings, resulting in Victoria's first vintage in 1845.

Today, **Yering Station** ❶ (38 Melba Highway, Yarra Glen; tel: 9730 0100; www.yering.com; Mon–Fri 10am–5pm, Sat–Sun 10am–6pm) continues its winemaking tradition and welcomes

visitors to its cellar door, housed in an 1859 building. There's also a magnificently sited wine bar-restaurant-art gallery that sits in attractive landscaped gardens. On the third Sunday of every month, the property's historic barn hosts the **Yarra Valley Regional Farmers' Market** (tel: 9739 0122; www.yarravalleyfood.com.au; 9am–2pm).

TARRAWARRA MUSEUM OF ART

Leave Yering Station, drive to Yarra Glen and turn right into the Healesville–Yarra Glen Road. After approximately 7km (4 miles) you will come to the **TarraWarra Museum of Art ❷** (no. 311; tel: 5957 3100; www.twma.com.au; Tue–Sun 11am–5pm; charge) on the right-hand side.

Set in an award-winning vineyard, this is one of Australia's most impressive contemporary art galleries, notable for its elegant purpose-designed building by local architect Alan Powell

and for the fact that it is a privately funded institution. The curators here draw on the many significant works of Australian contemporary art collected by owners Eva and Marc Besen when putting together the gallery's changing exhibition programme, also accessing works from other notable collections around the country.

There's a stylish wine bar here where you can enjoy tastings of TarraWarra's excellent vintages (try the Chardonnay and Pinot Noir) or sit down for a meal.

HEALESVILLE

From TarraWarra, continue along the Healesville–Yarra Glen Road until you reach a fork in the road. Turn right to visit the pretty town of **Healesville ❸**, nestled in the foothills of the Great Dividing Range. Settled during the gold rush, it is now a somewhat sleepy nook that's nudged fully awake only at weekends, when it is inundated with day-trippers from Melbourne.

Above from far left: a Yarra Valley wine estate; enjoying a TarraWarra pinot noir.

Valley Ballooning Companies offering early-morning hot-air balloon flights over the Yarra Valley include Balloon Sunrise (www.hotairballooning.com.au) and Global Ballooning (www.globalballooning.com.au).

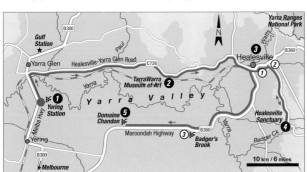

Above from left:
bottles of red at Giant Steps; Victoria's spectacular coastline.

Below: koala at Healesville Sanctuary.

LUNCH OPTIONS

If you are keen to picnic somewhere in the valley, the best place for provisions is **Kitchen & Butcher**, see ①①. For a slap-up lunch accompanied by a glass of a local tipple, your best option is to head northeast along the Maroondah Highway to the **Giant Steps/Innocent Bystander Winery**, see ①②, which has an award-winning pizzeria/café. Alternatively, veer southwest along the same highway to reach the fabulous **Bella Vedere** restaurant, see ①③.

HEALESVILLE SANCTUARY

The **Healesville Sanctuary** ❹ (tel: 5957 2800; www.zoo.org.au/Heales ville; daily 9am–5pm; charge) is on the southeastern edge of the town. To get there, turn into Badger Creek Road just to the east of the town centre. Home to more than 200 species of Australian birds, mammals and reptiles, this bushland reserve offers close-up encounters with indigenous cuties such as koalas, kangaroos, wombats and emus.

DOMAINE CHANDON

From Healesville, drive southeast along the Maroondah Highway to come to one of the valley's most spectacularly sited wineries – **Domaine Chandon** ❺ (no. 727, Coldstream; tel: 9378 9200; www.domainechandon.com.au; daily 10.30am–4.30pm). It's only a couple of kilometres on from Bella Vedere.

Established by French champagne house Moët & Chandon in 1986 in acknowledgement of the fact that the valley offers climatically perfect conditions in which to produce sparkling wines, the winery offers free 30-minute **guided tours** at 11am, 1pm and 3pm daily and a two-hour **wine discovery class** on Sundays, 11am–1pm (bookings essential; tel: 9738 9245; charge). End the tour with a glass of bubbly in the winery's spectacular Green Point Brasserie.

GREAT OCEAN ROAD

Along with Uluru, the Sydney Opera House and the Great Barrier Reef, Victoria's Great Ocean Road is one of Australia's major tourism icons. This excursion highlights its spectacular scenery and world-famous beach culture.

Begun in 1919 and finished in 1932, the Great Ocean Road was built by 3,000 ex-servicemen ('diggers') who had returned to Australia from overseas duty in World War I. It was conceived as a lasting memorial to their many colleagues who lost their lives fighting in the conflict. Using only picks, shovels and horse-drawn carts, the diggers carved the 243km (151-mile) road out of rock, dense bushland and forest.

Today, the road is known as one of the world's great coastal drives, and the journey from Torquay to Allansford, near Warrnambool, offers spectacular natural scenery, delicious food and wine stops and adrenalin-inducing activities aplenty.

WERRIBEE PARK

Only a 30-minute drive from central Melbourne, **Werribee Park** ❶ (K Road, Werribee; tel: 131 963; www. werribeepark.com.au; Oct–Apr Mon–Fri 10am–6.30pm, Sat–Sun 10am–5pm, other months 10am–4pm; free) is a fascinating first stop on this incursion into the state of Victoria's western districts.

DISTANCE 34km (21 miles) from central Melbourne to Werribee Park, plus approximately 270km (167 miles) for this tour and 240km (149 miles) back
TIME Three days
START Werribee Park
END Port Campbell National Park
POINTS TO NOTE
It is recommended to rent a car for this excursion. From Melbourne, take the Westgate Freeway (M1) and continue west on the Princes Freeway (M1) before leaving the freeway at the Werribee South/Werribee Park exit and following the signs to Werribee Park Mansion. From Werribee Park, rejoin the M1 and continue west for 30 minutes to Geelong. From Geelong, take the Surfcoast Highway (B100) to access the Great Ocean Road. In summer, book accommodation and restaurants well in advance. Bellbrae Harvest Restaurant, Qdos Arts, Chris's Restaurant and the Cape Otway Light Station all offer accommodation.

Public Transport
To do this trip on public transport, you will need to use a range of services. To get to Werribee Park from central Melbourne, catch the Werribee Park Shuttle Service (tel: 9748 5094; www. werribeeparkshuttle. com.au), which leaves daily at 9.20am from the National Gallery of Victoria. Bookings are essential. From Werribee Park, catch a taxi or bus no. 439 to Werribee Station, from where you can catch a V/Line train (www. vline.com.au) to Geelong. From Geelong Station V/Line coaches travel to Apollo Bay via Torquay, Anglesea, Aireys Inlet and Lorne. From Apollo Bay, a different V/Line coach travels to Port Campbell and on to Warrnambool, from where trains travel to Melbourne (www.met linkmelbourne.com.au.

Swimming Safety

Werribee Park Mansion

Built for pastoralist Thomas Chirnside, the 60-room **Werribee Park Mansion** dates from 1873–8. It is the most impressive of the many country residences built in the 19th century by the wealthy local landowners and pastoralists known as the 'squattocracy'. An interesting audiotour gives a glimpse of how life was in the mansion's heyday.

A walk around the extensive **formal gardens** is a highlight, particularly as the estate is the home of the well-respected Helen Lempriere National Sculpture Award (www.lempriere. perpetual.com.au) – winning entries from past years are scattered along formal walks, on the sweeping lawns and around the ornamental lake. Between November and April, the bushes in the adjacent **Victoria State Rose Garden** (daily 9am–5.30pm) are in full and wonderfully fragrant bloom.

In 1923 the property was acquired by the Catholic Church, which used it as a seminary. The Church built several new wings, including one now occupied by the **Mansion Hotel and Spa**. Its **Joseph's Restaurant**, see ①①, is an excellent spot for lunch.

Werribee Open Range Zoo

After lunch, consider visiting the **Werribee Open Range Zoo** (tel: 9731 9600; www.zoo.org.au; daily 9am–5pm; charge), home to rhinos, giraffes, zebras, hippos, lions, cheetahs and monkeys living in an environment designed to resemble the African savannah.

GEELONG

Continue west along the M1 for 40km (25 miles) to Victoria's second-largest

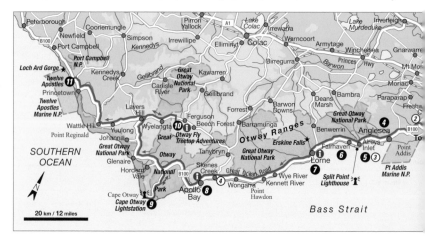

city. **Geelong ❷** is best-known as the gateway to the state's famous Surf Coast, but its long history and picturesque location on Corio Bay mean that it's worth a brief stop en route. Its name derives from Jillong, the local Wathaurong people's word for 'land' or 'cliffs'. When you enter town, follow the road signs towards the city centre and park in the vicinity of the Geelong Performing Arts Centre.

Geelong Gallery

The **Geelong Gallery** (Little Malop Street; tel: 5229 3645; www.geelong gallery.org.au; daily 10am–5pm; guided tours Sat 2pm; free), situated opposite the Performing Arts Centre, has a well-respected permanent collection that includes highlights such as the 1856 painting *View of Geelong* by Eugène von Guérard and Frederick McCubbin's moving 1890 work *A Bush Burial*, one of the gallery's first acquisitions.

Waterfront

From the gallery, walk north along Gheringhap Street to reach the historic waterfront precinct, which has undergone an extensive refurbishment programme over the past decade.

To the right of Cunningham Pier you will find the city's popular **Carousel** (1 Eastern Beach Road; tel: 5224 1547; Oct–Mar Mon–Fri 10.30am–5pm, Sat until 8pm, Sun until 6pm, Apr–Sept Mon–Fri 11am–4.30pm, Sat 10.30am–6pm, Sun 10.30am–5pm; charge), a steam-driven gem built in New York in 1892 and now housed in a modern glass pavilion.

As you walk east to the Eastern Beach Reserve you will pass a troop of colourful **baywalk bollards** painted

Above from far left: colourful bollards at Geelong; Werribee Park Mansion; the Cunningham Pier sign.

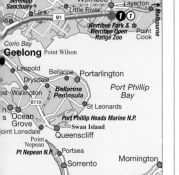

Food and Drink 🍴

① JOSEPH'S RESTAURANT
Mansion Hotel and Spa, Werribee Park, K Road, Werribee; tel: 9731 4000; www.lancemore. com.au; daily 6.30–10.30am, noon–2.30pm and 6.30–10.30pm; $$$

Settings don't come much better than this, and fortunately the menu and wine list at this hotel restaurant live up to the surroundings. The set lunch menus are extraordinarily good value, and afternoon tea is served daily in the foyer between 3–5pm.

Surfing Lessons

If you are keen to take a surf lesson, local companies Torquay Surfing Academy (www.torquaysurf. com.au), Great Ocean Road Surf Tours (www.gorsurftours. com.au) and Westcoast Adventure & Surf School (www.westcoast adventure.org) offer classes in Torquay and Anglesea.

by local artist Jan Mitchell. At the reserve, an Art Deco **swimming enclosure** (including pavilion and youngsters' pool) takes pride of place.

TORQUAY

Leaving Geelong, take the Surf Coast Highway and drive south for approximately 25 minutes (18km/11 miles) until you arrive at **Torquay ❸**, touted as the 'birthplace of the global surf industry'. Famous for its surf beaches – including the world-renowned breaks Winki Pop and Bells – this rapidly growing town is where global brands such as Rip Curl and Quiksilver originated and where the **Rip Curl Pro Surf and Music Festival** (www.live.rip curl.com or www.ripcurl.com.au) is held each Easter. There are safe swimming beaches for families at Cosy Corner *(see margin, p.92)* and Fisherman's Beach, and Torquay and Jan Juc beaches offer perfect conditions for novice surfers.

Surfworld

Also here is the world's largest surfing museum, **Surfworld** (Surf City Plaza, Beach Road; tel: 5261 4606; www.surf world.com.au; daily 9am–5pm; charge). Full of surfing artefacts and memorabilia, the museum is home to the Australian Surfing Hall of Fame and a cinema screening surfing films. The **Torquay Visitor Information Centre** (tel: 1800 620 888; http://visitgreat oceanroad.org.au; daily 9am–5pm) is next door.

ANGLESEA TO FAIRHAVEN

The Great Ocean Road officially starts at Torquay. Follow the highway signs to Anglesea, a 20-minute drive through bushland. For a memorable meal en route, turn off the Great Ocean Road at Gundrys Road, take the first right and then the first left to reach **Bellbrae Harvest Restaurant**, see ⑪②.

Anglesea

Known for its wide front beach, sheer cliffs and coastal heathland, **Anglesea ❹** is surrounded by national parkland and is a hive of activity during summer,

---

Food and Drink 🍴

② BELLBRAE HARVEST RESTAURANT

45 Portreath Road, Bellbrae; tel: 5266 2100; http://bellbrae harvestrestaurant.com.au; Fri noon–3pm, Fri–Sat dinner from 5pm, Sat–Sun 9.30–11.30am, noon–3pm; $$
In summer outdoor tables overlook a picturesque dam; in winter meals are served in front of an open fire. Bellbrae's innovative menu travels the globe, and does so utilising the very best of local ingredients along the way.

③ A LA GRÈCQUE

60 Great Ocean Road, Aireys Inlet;
www.alagrecque.com.au; tel: 5289 6922; Dec–Mar daily 9am–11.30am, 12.30–2.30pm, 6–10pm (off season Apr–Nov Wed–Sun, closed mid-June–mid-Aug); $$
There are no views on offer at this hugely popular taverna, just stylish surroundings and an unpretentious and delicious Greek and Mediterranean-flavoured menu. Owners Pam and Kosta Talimanidis have been operating restaurants along the coast for decades. It's also a popular coffee stop.

when thousands of families from Melbourne pack their boogie boards and bathers and make the pilgrimage here for their annual beach holiday.

Respected local outfit **Eco-Logic Environmental Services** (3 Camp Road; tel: 5263 1133; www.ecologic. net.au; charge) offers activities including snorkel tours, guided walks and rockpool rambles. If you play a round at the 18-hole **Anglesea Golf Club** (45 Golf Links Road; tel: 5263 1582; www.angleseagolfclub.com.au; daily 11am–sunset; charge), look out for the many kangaroos grazing nonchalantly on the course.

Aireys Inlet

From Anglesea, the road hugs the coastline and offers spectacular views. The next town is sleepy **Aireys Inlet** ❺, home to the landmark Split Point Lighthouse and excellent **A La Grècque** restaurant, café and bar, see ⑪③. An easy and clearly signed 3.5km (2-mile) clifftop walk starts near the lighthouse and offers wonderful coastal views.

Fairhaven

Adjacent to Aireys Inlet is the exclusive hamlet of **Fairhaven** ❻, where huge privately owned beach properties are scattered throughout native bushland. The surf beach here is one of the most beautiful – and unpredictable – in Victoria. Only swim here if lifesavers are on duty. From Fairhaven, it's a winding 20-minute drive to the next stop, Lorne.

LORNE

Set between the sparkling waters of Loutit Bay and the forests of the Otway Ranges, **Lorne** ❼ is the most popular holiday destination on the Great Ocean Road. This means that it is packed with facilities, but can also be horrendously crowded. The beach here is perfect for families *(see margin, p.92)*, with gentle waves lapping a wide stretch of golden sand, and the main street is crammed with cafés, shops and a cinema. Once a year the town's pier is the starting point for a popular swimming competition *(see margin)*.

Qdos Arts

To escape from the mayhem, consider enjoying breakfast, coffee or lunch at **Qdos Arts** (35 Allenvale Road; tel: 5289 1989; www.qdosarts.com; Thur–Mon 9am–5.30pm, Tue and Wed holiday periods only), an attractive complex set in tranquil bushland on the hill behind town. It comprises an art gallery, pottery studio, treehouse accommodation and café-restaurant.

To get there, turn left at the roundabout next to the **Lorne Visitor Information Centre** (15 Mountjoy Parade; tel: 1800 620 888; http://visit greatoceanroad.org.au; daily 9am–5pm) and drive up Otway Street until you reach a roundabout at the top of the hill. Allenvale Road is the second exit from the roundabout.

Headline Acts
In summer Lorne plays host to two popular events. During the New Year holiday period, the Falls Music and Arts Festival (www.falls festival.com), one of Australia's most popular live-music events, is held near Erskine Falls. And a week or so later, the famous Pier to Pub open water swim (www.lornesurfclub. com.au) attracts 4,000 swimmers from around Australia and overseas.

Erskine Falls

From Lorne, you can also enjoy bush walks in the nearby national park. The most popular of these is to dramatic **Erskine Falls**, a series of waterfalls cascading into a beautiful gully filled with native tree ferns. To access the falls, drive up Otway Street, turn right at William Street and continue into Erskine Falls Road. The falls are a 20-minute hike down a steep staircase.

LORNE TO APOLLO BAY

Having left Lorne, you will come to the most stunning section of the Great Ocean Road, with sheer cliffs and majestic ocean views on one side and the Great Otway National Park on the other. After passing through the holiday hamlets of Wye River and Kennett River, you will reach Skenes Creek and the neighbouring town of

Apollo Bay after an hour's drive. This winding and dangerous stretch of road is exhausting to drive, so when you reach **Skenes Creek**, consider resting over a meal at the magnificently located **Chris's Restaurant**, see ④, which offers panoramic views of the coastline. **Apollo Bay** ❽ is a popular, unpretentious resort with great beaches.

GREAT OTWAY NATIONAL PARK

The **Great Otway National Park** covers 103,000ha (255,000 acres) of ancient rainforest, heathlands and woodlands. The most spectacular stretch of the park begins approximately 6km (3¹⁄₄ miles) west of Apollo Bay. Popular walks include the Triplet Falls, Stevenson's Falls and Little Aire walks, the Distillery Creek Circuit and the Great Ocean Walk. For details, contact the **Parks Victoria Information Centre** (tel: 131 963; www.park web.vic.gov.au) or the **Great Ocean Road Visitor Centre** at Apollo Bay (100 Great Ocean Road; tel: 1800 620 888; http://visitgreatoceanroad.org.au; daily 9am–5pm).

Cape Otway Lightstation

The **Cape Otway Lightstation** ❾ (Great Ocean Road, Cape Otway; tel: 5237 9240; www.lightstation.com; daily 9am–5pm; charge) is a 30-minute drive from Apollo Bay, veering left off

Loch Ard **Shipwreck**
The Loch Ard Gorge 5.5km (3½ miles) east of Port Campbell was the scene of a tragic shipwreck in 1878. Information panels at the gorge tell the gripping tale of the clipper *Loch Ard*, the 52 passengers who drowned when it was wrecked on the reef and the two young people who survived.

> **Food and Drink** 🍴
> **④ CHRIS'S RESTAURANT**
> 280 Skenes Creek Road, Apollo Bay; tel: 5237 6411; www.chriss. com.au; daily 8.30–10am, noon–2pm and 6–10pm; $$$$
> Perched high in the Otways overlooking Bass Strait, Chris's is known throughout Australia for its spectacular setting and fresh seafood dishes, which are cooked simply but with great expertise. It is worth booking one of the villas to stay here overnight so that you can admire the sunset over dinner.

the Great Ocean Road after 18.5km (11½ miles) into the Otway Lighthouse Road. Constructed in 1848, it is the oldest surviving lighthouse in Australia. The station runs daily off-road Lightkeeper's Shipwreck Discovery tours at 10am–noon and 2–4pm and also offers accommodation in its historic lighthouse keepers' cottages. From May to October, it is a popular spot for whale spotting.

Otway Fly Treetop Walk

Approximately 54km/36 miles from Apollo Bay is the spectacular **Otway Fly Treetop Adventures** ❿ (tel: 1800 300 477; www.otwayfly.com; daily 9am–5pm; charge), a 600m (2,000ft) steel walkway perched 25m (80ft) high in the rainforest treetops, providing a walk within a canopy of myrtle beech, blackwood and mountain ash. To get there, turn into the Colac Road from Lavers Hill and follow the road signs.

PORT CAMPBELL NATIONAL PARK

Although it features on postcards and tourist brochures galore, no photographic image can do true justice to the utterly magnificent **Port Campbell National Park** (www.parkweb.vic. gov.au). This stretch of coastline from Princetown to Peterborough is best-known for the world-famous **Twelve Apostles** ⓫, giant rock stacks left

isolated from the mainland by the erosive power of the ocean. A visitor centre at the Twelve Apostles tells you about the geology and history of the area, and a tunnel under the Great Ocean Road leads to the viewing platforms. The rest of the coastline is home to blowholes, gorges, sea canyons and majestic cliffs.

From Port Campbell, the fastest return route to Melbourne is via the inland town of Colac. The trip will take you three hours.

Above: a pair of Apostles.

Below: fishing at Apollo Bay.

DIRECTORY

A user-friendly alphabetical listing of practical information,
plus hand-picked hotels and restaurants, clearly organised
by area, to suit all budgets and tastes. Select nightlife listings
are also included here.

A

AGE RESTRICTIONS

The age of consent for both hetero-sexual and homosexual sex in Victoria is 16. Drivers must be aged 18 to obtain a licence. The legal drinking age is 18.

B

BUDGETING

Accommodation. A bed at a back-packer hostel costs from A$25 a night, a room in a three star hotel costs around A$150 and a room in a four- or five-star hotel can start as low as A$200.

Restaurants. A main course costs around A$20 at a budget restaurant, A$25–30 at a mid-range restaurant and over A$40 at an expensive rest-aurant. A 285ml glass of beer costs around A$5–6 and a cup of tea or coffee is about A$3.50. A glass of house wine averages around A$8–10 in most bars and restaurants.

Car rental. Renting a small car starts at A$50 per day including taxes. Petrol (gasoline) is more expensive than in the US, but is considerably cheaper than in most European countries.

Airport taxi. A taxi between Mel-bourne Airport and central Melbourne will cost around A$55.

See Melbourne Attractions Pass. This gives the holder admission to more than 30 attractions in Mel-bourne as well as the surrounding regions. The card comes in two-, three- and seven-day versions, and can be purchased online (http://seemel bournepass.iventurecard.com) or at the Melbourne Visitor Centre at Fed-eration Square.

C

CLOTHING

'Four seasons in one day' is a statement regularly used to describe Melbourne's weather. Be ready for any conditions: a warm sweater is often needed in summer, and winter can call for heavy jackets, scarves and gloves. Bring an umbrella at every time of year, a rain-coat from April to September, and sunblock and a hat for summer. For climate information, *see p.12.*

CRIME AND SAFETY

Although Melbourne has a reputation as being a safe place in which to live and travel, you should use the same common sense and precautions as you would elsewhere regarding your pos-sessions and personal security. The nightclub precinct in central Mel-bourne and railway station platforms in the city centre and suburbs can be dangerous late at night, when excessive alcohol consumption sometimes trig-gers violent incidents. For details of inner-city police stations, *see p.105.*

CUSTOMS

Australia has extremely strict regulations about what can and cannot be brought into the country. Before disembarking from a plane, visitors are asked to fill in an Incoming Passenger Card. Australian customs officers check the information on the cards when passengers disembark and may initiate a baggage search. There are heavy fines for false or inaccurate claims, so it is always best to declare an item if in doubt. In addition, there are strict quarantine rules when entering and travelling between states.

Anyone over the age of 18 is allowed to bring into Australia A$900 worth of goods (not including alcohol or tobacco), 2,250ml (about 4 pints) of alcohol (wine, beer or spirits) and 250 cigarettes or 250g of cigars or tobacco products other than cigarettes. For more information, see www.customs.gov.au.

D

DISABLED TRAVELLERS

The **National Information Communications Awareness Network** (NICAN; tel: 1800 806 769; www. nican.com.au) is a national organisation that keeps an online database of facilities and services with access for the disabled, including accommodation and tourist sights.

Low-floor trams and buses suitable for wheelchairs are gradually being introduced to Melbourne's public transport system. For details of accessible stops and services, go to www.transport.vic.gov.au/doi/internet/transport.nsf and click on the Accessibility of Public Transport link.

The **Melbourne Mobility Centre** (1st Floor, Federation Square Car Park, corner Russell and Flinders streets; tel: 1800 735 266, TTY 9650 9316; www. accessmelbourne.vic.gov.au; Mon–Fri 9am–6pm, Sat–Sun 10am–4pm) offers services such as wheelchair hire, information for visitors with disabilities, fully accessible toilets and TTY telephone.

There are **Travellers Aid Centres** (tel: 9654 2600; www.travellersaid. org.au) at the Flinders Street and Southern Cross stations. These offer accessible toilets with hoist and adult change tables, toileting assistance, wheelchair hire and recharging, and communication assistance.

Most of the large tourist attractions are wheelchair-accessible.

E

ELECTRICITY

The current is 240/250v, 50Hz, and Australia uses 'type I' plugs with a grounding pin and two flat prongs forming a V shape. Most hotels have universal outlets for 110v shavers and small appliances.

Above from left: part of the *Federation Tapestry* in the Melbourne Museum *(see p.51)*, commissioned to mark the 2001 centenary of the Federation; *The Australian* and *The Financial Review* are Australia's two national dailies.

EMBASSIES AND CONSULATES

British Consulate General, 17th Floor, 90 Collins Street, Melbourne 3000; tel: 9652 1600 (office hours); http://ukinaustralia.fco.gov.uk; Mon–Fri 10am–12.30pm and 1.30–4pm.

Visa and passport enquiries should be made to the **British High Commission** in Canberra: Commonwealth Avenue, Yarralumla, ACT 2600; tel: 1902 941 555; Mon–Fri 9am–5pm.

Consulate of Canada, Level 27, 101 Collins Street, Melbourne (by appointment); tel: 9653 9674; www.canada.org.au.

Visa and passport enquiries should be made to the **Consulate General of Canada**: Level 5, 111 Harrington Street, Sydney, NSW 2000; tel: 02-9364 3000; Mon–Fri 8.30am–4.30pm.

Embassy of Ireland, 20 Arkana Street, Yarralumla, ACT 2600, Canberra; tel: 02-6214 0000; www.embassyofireland. au.com; Mon–Thur 9.30am–12.45pm and 2–5pm, Fri 2–4pm..

Consulate General of the United States, 553 St Kilda Road, Melbourne 3004; tel: 9526 5900; http://melbourne. usconsulate.gov; Mon–Fri 9am–4pm.

EMERGENCIES

For police, fire or ambulance, call **000**.

G

GAY AND LESBIAN TRAVELLERS

Melbourne has a thriving gay scene. Clubs and bars are clustered in the inner-northern suburbs of Fitzroy, Collingwood and Abbotsford and Prahran. The suburb of Northcote, in the inner north, has a large lesbian community, and the suburbs of South Yarra, Prahran and St Kilda in the inner south are favoured by gay men. The age of consent for homosexual sex is 16.

To find out what's on in the city, pick up a copy of the free weekly publication *Melbourne Community Voice* (http://mcv.gaynewsnetwork. com.au) in cafés and bars around town. Alternatively, tune into JOY (94.9 FM), Melbourne's radio station for the gay, lesbian, bisexual, transgender and intersex community.

Each year, the Midsumma Festival (www.midsumma.org.au) celebrates gay culture through arts and sporting events, dance parties and a Pride March.

Gay and Lesbian Tourism Australia (www.galta.com.au) promotes gay-owned or gay-friendly accommodation and tour operators via its website.

GREEN ISSUES

Victorians take environmental issues seriously, and each of the three tiers of government offers programmes and

services to foster environmentally responsible behaviour. Due to the nationwide drought, water restrictions have been in place across the state since 2005 – when here, take short showers and don't leave taps running. Recycling of glass, plastic, aluminium and paper is widespread – look for recycling bins with yellow lids. For more information, see www.sustainability.vic.gov.au. For information on carbon-offsetting your flights, *see margin, right.*

H

HEALTH

Australia has excellent medical services. For medical attention outside of working hours, go to the casualty department of a major hospital, look for a medical practitioner in the *Yellow Pages* (www.yellowpages.com.au) or ask at your hotel for advice.

The biggest danger for travellers in Australia is the sun. Even on mild, cloudy days it has the potential to burn. Wear a broad-brimmed hat and, if you are planning on being out in the sun for a while, a long-sleeved shirt made from a light fabric. It is recommended that you wear SPF30+ sunblock at all times, even under a hat.

Inoculations. No vaccinations are required for entry to Australia.

Health care and insurance. The Australian Government has signed Reciprocal Health Care Agreements with the governments of the Republic of Ireland and New Zealand which entitle citizens of those countries to limited subsidised health services for medically necessary treatment while visiting Australia.

If you are a citizen of the United Kingdom you are entitled to the same limited subsidised health services for medically necessary treatment, and you are also entitled to Medicare benefits for out-of-hospital medical treatment provided by doctors through private surgeries and community health centres. Visitors from all other countries should organise their own private medical insurance.

Pharmacies and hospitals. The chemist (pharmacy) is a great place to go for advice on minor ailments such as bites and stomach troubles. If you have a prescription from your doctor, and you want to take it to a pharmacist in Australia, you will need to have it endorsed by a local medical practitioner.

HOURS AND HOLIDAYS

Shops usually open Mon–Fri 9am–5pm (often later) and weekends 10am–5pm. Late-night shopping occurs in the CBD on Thursdays and Fridays, with most stores open until 7pm or 9pm.

Public Holidays
1 Jan: New Year's Day
26 Jan: Australia Day/Invasion Day
2nd Mon in Mar: Labour Day

Carbon-Offsetting
Air travel produces a huge amount of carbon dioxide and is a significant contributor to global warming. If you would like to offset the damage caused to the environment by your flight, a number of organisations can do this for you using online 'carbon calculators' that tell you how much you need to donate. In the UK travellers can visit www.jpmorgan climatecare.com or www.carbonneutral. com; in the US log on to www.climate friendly.com or www.sustainable travelinternational.org.

Internet Facilities

Most Victorian households have home internet access, so there are very few internet cafés. The State Library of Victoria *(see p.46)* offers free internet access on 50 PCs in the second-floor Redmond Barry Reading Room (60-minute maximum) and on 50 PCs in the ground-floor Information Centre (15-minute maximum). The library also offers free WiFi.

Mar/Apr: Good Friday, Easter Saturday and Monday
25 Apr: Anzac Day
2nd Mon in June: Queen's Birthday
1st Tue in Nov: Melbourne Cup
25 Dec: Christmas Day
26 Dec: Boxing Day

When a public holiday falls on a weekend, the following Monday is declared a holiday.

LEFT LUGGAGE

Travellers Aid (Main Concourse, Flinders Street Station, Flinders and Swanston streets, between platforms 9 and 10; tel: 9610 2030; www.travellers aid.org.au; Sun–Thur 8am–8pm, Fri–Sat 8am–10pm) offers short-term luggage storage at reasonable rates. More expensive luggage lockers are available at **Southern Cross Railway Station** (tel: 9619 2588; www.southerncross station.net.au; open during train service times). At the airport, luggage storage is offered by **SmarteCarte** (daily 5am–12.30am), in the Arrivals Hall in Terminal 2.

MAPS

The Melbourne Visitor Centre at Federation Square stocks the free *Melbourne Official Visitors' Map*, covering the central city and the train and tram networks, plus free maps of regional Victoria. PDFs of transport maps are available at www.metlinkmelbourne. com.au/maps-stations-stops.

MEDIA

Print media. The city's major broadsheet is *The Age* (www.theage.com.au); tabloid readers opt for *The Herald Sun* (www.heraldsun.com.au). The two national dailies are *The Australian* (www.theaustralian.com.au) and *The Financial Review* (www.afr.com). Free street press includes *Beat* (www. beat.com.au) and *Inpress*, both good for entertainment listings. You can pick these up at pubs, cafés and music stores.

Radio and television. The Australian Broadcasting Corporation (ABC) runs four national television channels as well as an extensive network of local and national radio stations including Radio National (621 AM) and Melbourne-based 3LO (774 AM). Both offer excellent current affairs programmes and talkback. There's also Triple J (107.5 FM) for alternative music and Classic FM (105.9 FM).

Three commercial television broadcasters (Ten, Nine and Seven) offer news, drama, soaps and game shows.

Australia's free-to-air ethnic/multi-cultural broadcaster, SBS, offers many foreign-language films and documentaries, foreign news, international football and Australia's best world

news. SBS Radio (93.1 FM or 1224 AM) broadcasts programmes in a wide variety of languages.

Local community radio stations 3RRR (102.7 FM) and PBS (106.7 FM) have devoted followings.

MONEY

The five major banks are ANZ, Commonwealth, National Australia Bank, Westpac and Bendigo Bank. Trading hours are generally Mon–Thur 9am–4pm and Fri 9am–5pm. Some branches open on Saturday mornings.

Currency. The local currency is the Australian dollar (abbreviated as AUD$, A$ or simply $), made up of 100 cents. There are 5c, 10c, 20c, 50c, $1 and $2 coins and $5, $10, $20, $50 and $100 notes. Single cents apply to many prices, and in these cases the amount will be rounded down or up to the nearest 5c.

Credit cards. Visa and MasterCard are accepted almost everywhere; American Express and Diners Club aren't quite as welcome.

Cash machines. Bank branches and automatic teller machines (ATMs) are common throughout Melbourne. ATMs are 24hr and are networked with Cirrus, Maestro, Barclays and other networks, meaning that you can use them to access funds from overseas accounts.

Traveller's cheques. All well-known traveller's cheques can be exchanged

for cash at banks, five-star hotels and exchange bureaux.

Tipping. Tipping is not obligatory, but a small gratuity for good service will be appreciated. When paying for a taxi fare, it is customary to round up to the nearest dollar or two. Restaurants do not usually levy a service charge, so most people tip waiters 10 per cent of the bill for good service. Hotel porters will expect between A$2–5, depending on how much baggage you have.

Taxes. A 10 per cent Goods and Services Tax (GST) is automatically added to most purchases. Visitors who purchase goods with a total value of A$300 or more from any one accredited supplier within 30 days of departure from Australia are entitled to a refund under the Tourist Refund Scheme (TRS). Refunds can be claimed at the TRS booth located beyond customs at the airport. For more details, see www.customs.gov.au.

P

POLICE

In an emergency, call 000. At other times call the general enquiries number for **Victoria Police** (tel: 9247 6666; Mon–Fri 7am–7pm). There are two police stations in central Melbourne that are open 24 hours: **Melbourne East** (tel: 9637 1100; 226 Flinders Lane) and **Melbourne West** (tel: 9247 6491; 637 Flinders Street).

Above from far left: police cars; Webb Footbridge across the Yarra.

Lost Property
The loss or theft of valuables should be reported to the police immediately, as most insurance policies insist on a police report. To do this, call the numbers given under the Police heading *(see left)*. For property lost on the major airlines or bus and coach services, try the following numbers: Melbourne International Airport, tel: 9297 1805; Qantas Baggage Services, tel: 1300 306 980 or 8336 4100; Jetstar Baggage Services, tel: 1800 687 374; Virgin Australia, tel: 8346 2437 (international), 9339 1750 (domestic); Southern Cross Station Luggage Hall, tel: 9619 2588; Metro (trains), tel: 1800 696 3876; Yarra Trams, tel: 1800 800 166.

POST

The efficient postal system is operated by **Australia Post** (tel: 13 7678; www. auspost.com.au), a government-run business enterprise that franchises its storefront operations. Post offices are generally open Mon–Fri 9am–5pm. There are a number of post offices in the CBD, including at 250 and 410 Elizabeth Street, 246 Flinders Lane, 210 Lonsdale Street and 440 Collins Street.

You can buy stamps at all post offices and at some newsagents. For assured next-day delivery within Australia it is possible to buy special Express Post envelopes. Otherwise, mail takes between one and three days to be delivered.

The cost of overseas mail depends on the weight and size of the item. At the time of writing, it cost A$1.50 to send a postcard to Europe or the USA, and A$2.25 to send a letter weighing up to 50g. Standard overseas mail takes about a week to most destinations.

Post boxes are red (standard mail) and yellow (Express Post mail).

SMOKING

It is illegal to smoke inside restaurants, bars, pubs and clubs in Victoria. Many venues have outdoor areas where smoking is allowed. It is also illegal to smoke on covered train platforms and in bus and tram shelters.

T

TELEPHONES

The national code for Australia is 61 and the area code for Victoria is 03.

To call out of Australia, dial 0011 + country code + area code (drop the first 0) + main number. The country code for Ireland is 353, the UK is 44 and the US and Canada are 1.

Public phones are located outside post offices and major transport terminals in the CBD, as well as in many pubs. These operate with coins and phonecards; the latter are sold through newsagents, post offices and Telstra shops, and can be used to make interstate and international calls.

Mobile phones. All Australian mobile numbers have a four-digit prefix starting with 04. To use your mobile (cell) here, buy a local SIM card and top it up with prepaid calls. Providers include Virgin Mobile (www.virginmobile.com.au), Telstra (www.telstra.com), Optus (www. optus.com.au), Three (www.three.com. au) and Vodafone (www.vodafone.com. au). All have shops in the CBD.

TIME ZONES

Melbourne is on Eastern Australian Standard Time (EST), which is 10 hours ahead of Greenwich Mean Time and 15 hours ahead of New York. So when it is noon in Melbourne, it is 2am in London and 9pm in New York.

Daylight Saving operates from the start of October to the start of April. During this period, Melbourne is 11 hours ahead of London and 16 ahead of New York, making it 1am in London and 8pm in New York.

TOILETS

There are pay toilets in some CBD streets, but most locals take advantage of the free toilets in the Myer and David Jones department stores in the Bourke Street Mall, in pubs, at railway stations and in large fast-food restaurants. The department store toilets also offer baby-change tables.

TOURIST INFORMATION

For online information, go to the Tourism Victoria websites: www.visit victoria.com and www.visitmelbourne. com. It is also worth checking the Melbourne City Council tourism website: www.thatsmelbourne.com.au.

The extremely helpful **Melbourne Visitor Centre** (tel: 9658 9658; daily 9am–6pm) is located at the north-western corner of Federation Square. There is also a **Melbourne Visitor Booth** (Mon–Sat 9am–5pm, Sun 10am–5pm) in the Bourke Street Mall.

Red-jacketed volunteers known as City Ambassadors can be found on the streets from Monday to Saturday. They can help with directions, transport queries and tourism information.

TRANSPORT

The vast majority of visitors to Victoria arrive by air. But once in Melbourne, there are plenty of ways to get around.

Airports and Arrival

There are two airports: **Melbourne Airport** (tel: 9297 1600; www.mel bourneairport.com.au), which is 22km (14 miles) northwest of the city centre, and the much smaller **Avalon Airport** (tel: 1800 282 566; www.avalonairport. com.au), 55km (34 miles) southwest of the city centre on the road to Geelong.

A taxi to or from Melbourne Airport takes 20–30 minutes and costs around A\$50. To Avalon, the trip takes around 50 minutes and costs around A\$130.

Skybus (tel: 9335 2811; www.sky bus.com.au; adult A\$16 one way, A\$26 return) operates a daily 24-hour shuttle bus service between the Melbourne Airport and Southern Cross Railway Station. Buses depart every 10 minutes during the day and every 15–30 minutes overnight. It also offers a pick-up/drop-off service to city hotels. All you have to do is transfer onto a SkyBus Hotel Transfer mini-bus at Southern Cross station, after registering your hotel details at the Hotel Transfer booth.

Sita Coaches (tel: 9689 7999; www. sitacoaches.com.au/avalon; A\$20 one way, A\$36 return) offers a shuttle bus service meeting all arriving and departing Jetstar and Tiger Airways flights at Avalon Airport. The bus

drops passengers at Southern Cross Station or at city hotels (extra charge levied and online booking essential).

Public Transport

Melbourne's integrated public transport system is run by **Metlink** (tel: 131 638; www.metlinkmelbourne.com.au) and comprises trams, buses and trains. A good way to introduce yourself to its services and buy tickets is to visit the **MetShop** (Mon–Fri 9am–5.30pm, Sat 9am–1pm) on the ground floor of the Melbourne Town Hall, on the corner of Swanston and Little Collins streets.

Metcards (tickets) offer unlimited travel over various periods (eg two hours, one day, one week) and throughout the various zones of the city (zone 1 is big enough for most visitors' purposes). They can be used on metropolitan trams, buses and trains (excluding airport services).

Prices are cheaper if you purchase a multi-trip Metcard in advance; these are available from newsstands and convenience stores displaying the blue Metcard sign, train stations, the MetShop, the Melbourne Visitor Centre at Federation Square or online (http://store.metlinkmelbourne.com.au). Concessions are only available to holders of an approved Victorian Concession Card or children aged 14 and under.

Two-hour and one-day tickets can be purchased from machines on board trams, from bus drivers and from machines or ticket booths at railway stations. After you purchase a Metcard, you must validate it in the machine on board the bus or tram, or at the train station.

Free City Transport

The free City Circle tram operates in both directions around the outer edge of the CBD (including along Spring, La Trobe and Flinders streets). Old 'W'-class trams painted brown to be different to other services, they stop at the Docklands and close to major tourist attractions including Federation Square, Melbourne Aquarium and the Melbourne Museum.

The Melbourne City Tourist Shuttle is a free bus service that stops at key tourist attractions in and around the City of Melbourne. Find out more at www.thatsmelbourne.com.au/shuttle.

Taxis

You can hail one of Melbourne's yellow-coloured taxis in the street if its rooftop light is on. Alternatively, taxi ranks can be found at major hotels or busy locations such as train stations. A trip from one end of the CBD to the other costs around A$10. There are surcharges for phone bookings, and for trips between midnight and 5am, departing from the airport taxi rank and using the CityLink freeway or other tolls.

The major companies are **Silver Top Taxis** (tel: 131 008; www.silvertop.com.au) and **13 CABS** (aka Black Cabs, tel: 132 227; www.13cabs.com.au).

Driving

Traffic drives on the left in Australia. Most of Victoria's road regulations are based on international rules, and it is simply a matter of following the signs and sticking to the speed limits. Vic Roads (www.vicroads.vic.gov.au) can provide information about road rules.

The speed limit in built-up city and suburban areas is 40kph (25mph), 50kph (30mph) or 60kph (38mph). On country roads it is 100kph (60mph) unless otherwise indicated.

There is a 0.05 per cent blood alcohol limit for drivers, which is widely enforced by the use of random breath tests carried out by the police. Random drug tests are also used.

Car rental. To rent a car for excursions into regional Victoria, you must be over 25 and possess a full licence in your country of origin. You will need a copy of the licence in English or an International Driving permit, your passport and a credit card to which a pre-authorised security bond can be charged. Drivers between 18 and 25 may be able to hire a vehicle if they pay a surcharge.

Car-rental firms with offices in central Melbourne and desks at the airports include **Avis** (tel: 136 333; www.avis.com.au), **Budget** (tel: 1300 362 848; www.budget.com.au), **Europcar** (tel: 1300 131 390; www.europcar.com.au) and **Thrifty** (tel: 1300 367 227; www.thrifty.com.au).

Car parks. There are many multi-storey car parks in the CBD, as well as street parking. Parking inspectors are very diligent about ticketing cars whose meters have expired.

VISAS AND PASSPORTS

Foreign nationals entering Australia must have a passport valid for the entire period of their stay and must have obtained a visa before leaving home (except for New Zealand citizens, who are issued with a visa on arrival in Australia). The Electronic Transfer Authority (ETA) visa is available to citizens of over 30 countries and can be obtained on the spot from travel agents or airline offices for a service charge of A$20. ETA visas are generally valid for 12 months; single stays must not exceed three months, but return visits within the 12-month period are allowed.

Most EU citizens are eligible for an eVisitor visa, which is free and can be obtained online.

Tourist visas are available for citizens of all countries for continuous stays of three, six or twelve months. You can apply for one of these online; a charge may be levied whether your application is successful or not.

Visitors travelling on ETAs, eVisitor visas and tourist visas are not permitted to work while in Australia.

For more information and to apply for visas online, go to www.immi.gov.au.

Above from far left: Melbourne's taxis are yellow; laneway graffiti.

Melbourne offers the full gamut of accommodation types, but is particularly blessed when it comes to apartment and boutique hotels. The best location in which to stay is the city centre or edge, although St Kilda and South Yarra both have their allure – St Kilda is particularly beloved by backpackers and South Yarra is the location of choice for visiting celebs. In the CBD, the best hotels tend to be located on or around Collins, Little Collins and Queen streets, although there are also attractive options scattered across the grid and on the East Melbourne, Fitzroy and Carlton fringes.

Last-minute accommodation is usually available, the only exception being when high-profile sporting festivals and events, such as the Australian Open (January), Australian Grand Prix (March), AFL Grand Final (September) and Spring Racing Carnival (November), are being held; at these times room rates rise and available rooms can be scarce, meaning that you should book well in advance.

Central Melbourne

The Adelphi

187 Flinders Lane; tel: 8080 8888; www.adelphi.com.au; $$$–$$$$

When it opened in 1990, this boutique hotel was as glam as they come. A showcase of the trademark visual style of local architectural doyens Denton Corker Marshall (who designed the Melbourne Museum), it is particularly notable for a whimsical rooftop lap pool, which is cantilevered over the street. Although the interior is looking a bit on the dated side these days, the rooftop bar and basement restaurant *(see p.116)* retain their hip credentials.

Alto Hotel on Bourke Street

636 Bourke Street; tel: 8608 5500; www.altohotel.com.au; $$$–$$$$

Close to Southern Cross Railway Station and the Docklands, Alto Hotel markets itself as being environmentally friendly. Its emissions are offset, 'green-choice' electricity is used, rainwater is utilised for cleaning, plastics are kept to a minimum and waste is recycled. Rooms and apartments have a warm colour scheme and bathrooms have granite features; apartments have a kitchenette. The cosy lounge, bar-restaurant and relaxation room give the place an edge.

City Centre Hotel

22 Little Collins Street; tel: 9654 5401; www.citycentrebudget hotel.com.au; $–$$

Price for a double room for one night without breakfast:

$$$$	over A$220
$$$	A$150–220
$$	A$80–150
$	below A$80

This family-run backpacker joint is in the midst of one of the most happening bar enclaves in the city, close to Parliament Station and the Treasury Gardens. There's free WiFi and internet, a roof terrace and laundry facilities. Rooms have a television, fridge, fans (no air-conditioning) and tea-and-coffee-making facilities; bathrooms are shared.

Crown Metropol

8 Whiteman Street, Southbank; tel: 9292 8888; www.crown metropol.com.au; $$$$

If a contemporary luxury hotel is what you're looking for, this is where you should be staying. Pamper yourself in the exclusive day spa, Isika, catch the breathtaking city views from 28, the sky bar on that level or take the plunge in one of the infinity pools.

Greenhouse Backpackers Melbourne

228 Flinders Lane; tel: 1800-249 207; www.friendlygroup.com.au; $

The institutional atmosphere won't be for everyone, but this no-nonsense backpacker joint near Flinders Street Railway Station offers the cheapest singles accommodation in the central city (couples might want to shop around for a cheaper and more comfortable alternative). There's key-card access for every room and the hostel is next to a 24-hour police station, so it is as safe and secure as they come. It also offers free internet access and a self-catering kitchen.

Hilton Melbourne South Wharf

2 Convention Centre Place, South Wharf; tel: 9027 2000; www.hiltonmelbourne.com.au; $$$$

This hotel's 396 rooms feature floor-to-ceiling windows with views of the city and the Yarra River. stylish Sotano Wine + Tapas was awarded Bar of the Year at the AHA Awards (2010), while Nuevo37 serves Spanish-inspired Australian fare.

Hotel Lindrum

26 Flinders Street; tel: 9668 1111; www.hotellindrum.com.au; $$$$

Once home to a well-known billiard hall, this attractive building is now one of the city's best boutique hotels. Close to Federation Square, it is within easy access of both CBD amenities and the sporting precinct along the Yarra. The hotel's 59 rooms and suites are as stylish as they are spacious; the de luxe versions also offer great views. There's a sleek restaurant and bar on the ground floor where you can relax after a day's exploration.

Hotel Windsor

111 Spring Street; tel: 9633 6000; www.thewindsor.com.au; $$$$

Gentility is the word that springs to mind when this grande dame of the city's hostelries is mentioned, and

Above from far left: The Prince, St Kilda *(see p.115)*; clean lines at Jasper Hotel *(see p.112)*.

although the possibility of a hip renovation has been much discussed, traditional decor and service currently reign supreme. Located opposite Parliament House, the hotel's rooms and public spaces are conservatively decorated and will please most guests. The traditional afternoon tea served daily in the lounge is a Melbourne institution. *See also p.36.*

Jasper Hotel

489 Elizabeth Street; tel: 8327 2777; www.jasperhotel.com.au; $$–$$$

Once the worthy but drab YWCA, the Jasper opened in 2007 after a huge renovation and now sports a rich colour scheme and funky aesthetic, making its claim to the boutique tag credible if not compelling. The hotel's location next to popular Queen Victoria Market *(see p.39)* is vibrant during the day but quiet at night.

The Langham Melbourne

One Southgate Avenue, Southbank; tel: 8696 8888; http://melbourne. langhamhotels.com.au; $$$$

One of the most lauded luxury hotels in Melbourne, The Langham has innovative facilities such as Service Stylists, paying attention to every detail. Having been around since 1865, the brand is also known for its excellent service. The hotel overlooks the Yarra River and is surrounded by countless dining and shopping options.

Mercure Welcome Melbourne

265 Little Bourke Street; tel: 9639 0555; www.accorhotels.com.au; $$–$$$

No boutique or luxury credentials here, just clean, neat and well-equipped rooms in a central location. The major department stores are around the corner, and the city's major tram route is directly in front of the hotel, making trips around Melbourne easy as pie. Check for on-line specials – they can be half the rack rate.

Park Hyatt

1 Parliament Square, off Parliament Place; tel: 9224 1234; www.melbourne.park.hyatt.com; $$$$

The central yet secluded location of this luxury pile opposite St Patrick's Cathedral almost seems at odds with its ostentatious decor, which looks to Las Vegas for inspiration. All is forgiven, though, when the spacious rooms with their king-sized beds and Italian marble baths are inspected.

Price for a double room for one night without breakfast:	
$$$$	over A$220
$$$	A$150–220
$$	A$80–150
$	below A$80

Facilities – including a well-equipped gym, indoor swimming pool, spa and excellent restaurant – are among the best in town.

Punt Hill Little Bourke

11–17 Cohen Place; tel: 1300 731 299; www.littlebourke.punthill. com.au; $$$

This attractive modern building in Melbourne's Chinatown offers comfortable apartments with kitchenettes and laundry facilities, while public facilities include a gym and an indoor lap pool. As befits the location, the building has been designed to meet feng shui requirements and there's a ground-floor Chinese restaurant. Melbourne's major theatres are only a curtain call away.

Robinsons in the City

405 Spencer Street; tel: 9329 2552; www.robinsonsinthecity.com.au; $$$–$$$$

Housed in an 1850s building that was Melbourne's first commercial bakery, this B&B on the edge of the city centre offers an intimate accommodation experience. Of the six rooms on offer, five have private bathrooms opposite the bedroom and one has an attached en-suite; all have free WiFi and air-conditioning. Breakfast is prepared by the owner and served in the old bakehouse. The location can be a little bit off-putting at night.

The Sebel Melbourne

394 Collins Street; tel: 9211 6600; www.mirvachotels.com/sebel-melbourne; $$$$

Spacious rooms and a prestigious Collins Street address await at this popular apartment hotel. The apartments are equipped with ergonomic work desks, kitchenettes and laundry facilities, and there's an on-site gym for the athletically inclined. Others may prefer to take advantage of the hotel's close proximity to Café Vue *(see p.31)*, which serves one of the best breakfasts in the city.

Sofitel Melbourne on Collins

25 Collins Street; tel: 9653 0000; www.sofitelmelbourne.com.au; $$$$

Located in the 'Paris End' of Collins Street, the Sofitel has rooms starting on level 36 of a high-rise tower. All rooms have spectacular views; if your budget allows, opt for a luxury room or a suite, as the standard room is slightly cramped. There are bars and restaurants galore, a business centre and a fitness centre.

Stamford Plaza

111 Little Collins Street; tel: 9659 1000; www.stamford. com.au; $$$$

Located at the top end of town, the Stamford Plaza has amenities aplenty, including an indoor/outdoor pool, a

Above from far left: sparkling Stamford Plaza; one of the Park Hyatt's spacious rooms.

restaurant, a bar and two gyms. All suites feature kitchenettes and bath-spas. The somewhat fussy decor here won't please fans of the minimalist aesthetic, but services such as complimentary overnight shoeshining may compensate.

Westin Melbourne

205 Collins Street; tel: 9635 2222; www.westin.com.au/melbourne; $$$$

The Westin has an outstanding location overlooking the City Square, St Paul's Cathedral and leafy Collins Street. Decor is stylishly understated, featuring muted colour schemes and excellent Australian contemporary art. The wellness centre features a lap pool, spa, gym and steam room. Top marks go to the bar and restaurant spaces that allow you to relax indoors or on a terrace overlooking the City Square.

Carlton and Parkville

Downtowner on Lygon

66 Lygon Street; tel: 9663 5555; www.downtowner.com.au; $$$

The location here is perfect – halfway between the city centre and the bohemian enclave of Carlton. Rooms are attractive and well equipped, with king-sized beds and small en-suites. Guests have free access to the Melbourne City Baths' pool and gym nearby. There's a restaurant and bar, but the Lygon Street alternatives are more alluring.

Fitzroy

The Nunnery

116 Nicholson Street; tel: 9419 8637; www.nunnery.com.au; $–$$

This place offers three tiers of accommodation and is deservedly popular. Housed in three historic buildings, its city-edge location faces the Carlton Gardens. The hostel occupies a former nunnery and offers a choice of budget single, double and dorm rooms, while the guesthouse has comfortable single, double and family rooms. At the top tier is the townhouse, with stylishly renovated singles and doubles. Bathrooms are shared, there are fans and heaters in all rooms and there's a communal kitchen and lounge in each building.

East Melbourne

Knightsbridge Apartments

101 George Street; tel: 9470 9100; www.knightsbridgeapartments.com.au; $$–$$$

In an excellent location close to Fitzroy Gardens, Melbourne Cricket Ground and the busy shopping and

Price for a double room for one night without breakfast:	
$$$$	over A$220
$$$	A$150–220
$$	A$80–150
$	below A$80

entertainment precinct of Bridge Road in Richmond, these serviced studio apartments offer WiFi, an en-suite bathroom, a kitchenette with basic equipment and air-conditioning. The decor is pleasant and rates are reasonable, particularly the last-minute deals.

Prahran, South Yarra and Toorak

The Como Melbourne

630 Chapel Street, South Yarra; tel: 9825 2222; www.mirvachotels.com/como-melbourne; $$$$

Many of the rich and famous wouldn't stay anywhere else. The Como offers suites with king-sized beds, spacious en-suites and sitting areas; some have private Japanese gardens while others have spas, balconies and study areas. There's an indoor/outdoor swimming pool, as well as a spa, sauna, gym and sundeck. Rates are extremely reason-able considering the level of service on offer, and the hotel's location is close to the shopping and eating temptations of Chapel Street and Toorak Road.

The Lyall

14 Murphy Street, South Yarra; tel: 9868 8222; www.thelyall.com; $$$$

This boutique hotel located on a leafy residential street off the upmarket South Yarra shopping and eating strip has the feel and decor of a pri-vate club. The suites feature elegant decor with plenty of luxurious touches – you are bound to sleep well here. The in-house spa, posh restau-rant and glam champagne bar ensure a sybaritic stay.

St Kilda

Base Backpackers Melbourne

17 Carlisle Street, St Kilda; tel: 8598 6200; www.stayatbase.com/base-backpackers-melbourne-hostel; $

This sleek operation markets itself as Australia's hippest hostel. Four- to eight-bed dorms have bunk beds, air-conditioning, security lockers and private en-suites; the 'Sanctuary Floor' is for females only. There are laundry facilities and an internet café, and St Kilda's lively café, bar and beach scene is right on the doorstep.

The Prince

2 Acland Street, St Kilda; tel: 9536 1111; www.theprince.com.au; $$$–$$$$

The über-stylish Prince was designed by the edgy architectural firm Wood Marsh and has worn well in the decade since it opened. Rooms feature de luxe linen, distinctive artwork and soothing colour schemes; the suites have fabu-lous views of Port Phillip Bay. The hotel's Aurora Spa is probably the best one in Melbourne, and the same encomium applies to the in-house Circa Restaurant.

Above from far left: hip hostel Base; Downtowner on Lygon.

Melbourne has one of the most impressive and diverse food scenes in the world – you will find every cuisine here to suit every budget. Most places are found in the city centre or inner suburbs, with hot spots being Fitzroy, St Kilda and East Brunswick (north of Carlton). The restaurants listed below are all extremely popular, so making a booking is highly recommended.

Central Melbourne

Becco

11–25 Crossley Street; tel: 9663 3000; www.becco.com.au; Mon–Sat noon–3pm and 6–11pm; $$$

This buzzy, stylish Italian restaurant-bar is tucked down a laneway at the eastern end of Bourke Street. It's hugely popular with city residents, who come to enjoy the home-style Italian cooking, including pasta classics and comfort mains such as *cotoletta* (crumbed veal cutlet). The bar serves inexpensive lunches during the day and tasty bar snacks at night.

Cookie

Level 1, Curtain House, 252 Swanston Street; tel: 9663 7660; www.cookie.net.au; daily noon–11pm (bar noon–3am); $

Boho Melbourne loves to drink at this excellent bar, and those in the know also eat their fill at Cookie's funky restaurant, where the inventive and tasty Thai cuisine pleases both palate and wallet. Don't expect a quiet or leisurely meal – this joint jumps, and staff will encourage you to kick on to the bar rather than linger at your table.

ezard

187 Flinders Lane: tel: 9639 6811; www.ezard.com.au; Mon–Fri noon–2.30pm and 6pm–late, Sat 6pm–late; $$$$

The sophisticated decor of this restaurant in the basement of the Adelphi hotel *(see p.110)* is more than matched by the menu, which features stunningly presented dishes conceived with confidence and executed with a great deal of skill. Owner/chef Teague Ezard uses the finest local produce, and has a particular love of Chinese and Thai-fusion styles, although he also flirts with Middle Eastern flavours.

Gingerboy

27–29 Crossley Street; tel: 9662 4200; www.gingerboy.com.au; Mon–Fri noon–2.30pm, Mon–Sat 6pm–late; $$

Southeast Asian hawker food gets a designer makeover here, complete with excellent cocktails and a wine list of Old and New World labels that harmonise well with the abundant hot, spicy, fishy and tangy flavours. The most notable of a spate of new and innovative Asian eateries in town.

Il Bàcaro

168 Little Collins Street; tel: 9654 6778; www.ilbacaro.com.au; Mon–

Above from far left: at the bar in MoVida; at work in a restaurant kitchen.

Sat noon–3pm and 6–10.30pm; $$$
With its sleek and sexy Italian decor, flirtatious Italian staff and skilfully cooked modern versions of classic Italian dishes, il Bàcaro has remained a perennial favourite on the Melbourne dining scene. The menu rarely surprises (neither does it disappoint), and the bar is a great spot for an *aperitivo*.

Longrain

44 Little Bourke Street; tel: 9671 3151; www.longrain.com.au; Fri noon–3pm, Mon–Fri 6–11pm, Sat 5.30–11pm, Sun 5.30–10pm; $$$
An outpost of the famous Sydney establishment, Longrain is known for its modern Thai-inspired cuisine. In a huge warehouse-style space in Chinatown, the restaurant's long and round communal tables are inevitably full of glamorous young things sharing a spicy meal together.

Merchant

Rialto 495 Collins Street; tel: 9614 7688; http://merchantov.com; Mon–Fri 7am–11pm, Sat noon–11pm; $$$
Chef Guy Grossi's latest restaurant housed in an old red brick building at the Rialto Towers forecourt is reminiscent of a vibrant and relaxed (but chic) restaurant in Venice. The hearty Northern Italian dishes include a huge range of risottos and polentas alongside grilled fresh seafood and meat. Finish off with gelato or a Venetian trifle.

MoVida

1 Hosier Lane; tel: 9663 3038; www.movida.com.au; daily noon–late; $$–$$$
One of the city's favourite eateries, Movida looks to Madrid for inspiration. Owner/chef Frank Camorra trained in Spain and delivers assured tapas and *raciones*, utilising a mix of top-quality local produce and the best Iberian imports. Dishes range from classic to unexpected, and are consistently delicious. If you have no luck scoring a table, try **Movida Next Door** (Corner Flinders Street and Hosier Lane; Fri noon–midnight, Tue–Thur 5pm–late; $$) or the newer and larger **Movida Aqui** (level 1, 500 Bourke Street; Mon–Fri noon–late, Sat 5pm–late; $$).

Sarti

6 Russell Place; tel: 9639 7822; www.sartirestaurant.com.au; Mon–Fri noon–3pm, Mon–Sat 6pm–late; $$$
The menu here has a classic Italian base but features some intriguing modern twists. The *stuzzichini* (small appetisers designed to be shared) are full of fun and flavour, the *paste* and *risotti* are

> Price guide for a two-course dinner for one with a glass of house wine:
>
> | | |
> |---|---|
> | $$$$ | over A$80 |
> | $$$ | A$60–80 |
> | $$ | A$45–60 |
> | $ | below A$45 |

refined and the mains inevitably incorporate an unusual ingredient or two. Best of all are the desserts, which are worth a visit in their own right.

Supper Inn
15 Celestial Avenue; tel: 9663 4759; daily 5.30pm–2.30am; $

The word 'institution' is often bandied around when talking about the city's eateries, but this is one of the few places that deserve to be described as such. Always crowded (particularly late at night), it has utterly wonderful Cantonese food that puts many of its more expensive neighbours to shame.

Taxi Dining Room
Level 1, Transport Hotel, Federation Square; www.transporthotel.com.au; tel: 9654 8808; daily noon–3pm and 6–11pm; $$$$

Locals wanting to impress clients or first dates head toward this stylish restaurant in Federation Square, which has one of the most stunning interiors in Melbourne. The impressive modern creations using Asian ingredients are complemented by an extraordinarily fine wine list.

Vue de Monde
430 Little Collins Street; tel: 9691 3888; www.vuedemonde.com.au; Tue–Fri, Sun noon–2pm, Mon–Sat 6–9.15pm; $$$$

Regularly nominated as one of Australia's two best restaurants, Shannon Bennett's Vue de Monde is not for diners after a low-key meal. The chef focuses on produce-driven cuisine using heirloom and organic vegetables and fruits sourced directly from growers and farmers as well as local and sustainable seafood and meat. The space at the top of the Rialto Towers afford a stunning view of the skyline and beyond.

Carlton, Parkville and East Brunswick

Abla's
109 Elgin Street, Carlton; tel: 9347 0006; www.ablas.com.au; Thur–Fri noon–3pm, Mon–Sat 6–11pm; $

Abla Amad's delectable home-style Lebanese food has devotees throughout the city. The dated interior hasn't a skerrick of the style sported by the trendy restaurants of Beirut, but the quality of her cooking would put most of those places to shame. The kibbe and kebabs are delicious, and the spiced pilaf with minced lamb, chicken and almonds is to die for.

Balzari
130 Lygon Street, Carlton; tel: 9639 9383; www.balzari.com.au; Tue–Fri noon–late, Sat–Sun 9.30am–late; $$

Balzari is a haven of style and good food wedged along the tatty tourist restaurants of Lygon Street. The menu takes inspiration from Northern Italy, featuring *risotti*, *paste*, meat and lots of seafood. The interior is modern and the service is unobtrusive but efficient.

Hellenic Republic

434 Lygon Street, East Brunswick; tel: 9381 1222; www.hellenic republic.com.au; Sat–Sun 9–11.30am, Fri–Sun noon–4pm, daily 5.30pm–late; $

Melbourne has the largest Greek population of any city outside Greece, so Greek restaurants here can hold their own with any in the old country. This taverna is owned by high-profile chef George Calombaris of Press Club fame *(see p.33)*, and is characterised by a casual atmosphere and a simple menu featuring fish, meat and salads.

Fitzroy

Añada

197 Gertrude Street, Fitzroy; tel: 9415 6101; www.anada.com.au; Mon–Fri 6pm–late, Sat–Sun noon–late; $

This place has an atmosphere and decor that immediately recall Spain, and a menu that could hold its own among the best tapas bars in Andalusia. Choose from an extensive list of simple but memorable tapas and *raciones*, and wash your choice down with a wine or sherry from Spain or Portugal.

Price guide for a two-course dinner for one with a glass of house wine:

$$$$ over A$80
$$$ A$60–80
$$ A$45–60
$ below A$45

Cutler & Co.

55–57 Gertrude Street; tel: 9419 4888; www.cutlerandco.com.au; Tue–Sun 6pm–late, Fri and Sun noon–11pm; $$–$$$

This highly acclaimed restaurant by Andrew McConnell has received rave reviews from critics for its wow factor. The space of an old metal work factory was transformed into the stylish dining room and bar. The food, perfectly balanced in taste and texture, is simple, fresh and fabulous.

Gigibaba

102 Smith Street, Collingwood; tel: 9486 0345; Tue–Sun 6–11pm; $

Ismail Tosun's modern takes on Turkish classics have the city's foodie fraternity frantically queuing for tables (there's a no-booking policy). His tapas-style dishes are sure to appeal to all palates, and the stylish fit out provides a funky feel. It's as far away from the staid Turkish restaurants of the suburbs as you could possibly imagine.

Ladro

224 Gertrude Street, Fitzroy; tel: 9415 7575; www.ladro.com.au, Sun noon–3pm, Mon–Fri 6–11pm, Sat–Sun 5.30–11pm; $

Melbourne's best pizza is on offer at this bustling and noisy place. The clientele matches the decor – arty chic – and eating here is very, very Melbourne. In winter the roasted meat of the day is popular, but what the

Above from far left: Hellenic Republic; unnecessary encouragement at Italian restaurant Sarti in the centre of town.

punters mainly come for are the thin-crust pizzas topped with delights such as potato and truffle oil.

The Yarra and Docklands

Giuseppe Arnaldo & Sons

Crown Casino, Southbank; tel: 9694 7400; www.idrb.com; daily noon–midnight; $$

The no-booking policy should have put off some of the city's notoriously fickle foodies, but even this hasn't stopped the crowds flocking to this huge and theatrical Italian eatery at the Crown Casino. The menu features classic Roman dishes and the wine list includes lots of well-priced Italian choices. The lack of natural light means that it's more suited to dinner than lunch.

Nobu Melbourne

Crown Complex, 8 Whiteman Street, Southbank; tel: 9292 7879; Mon–Thur noon–2.30pm. Fri–Sun noon–3pm, Sun–Thur 6–10.30pm, Fri–Sat 6–11pm; $$$$

Nobu's southern hemisphere outpost, just like the rest of his culinary empire,

is a glamorous and vibrant affair. The modern Japanese menu follows the Nobu formula of great ingredients and flavours. Try the signature black cod with miso or Nobu's creative version of fish and chips.

Prahran, South Yarra, Toorak and Windsor

The Argo

64 Argo Street, South Yarra; tel: 9867 3344; www.theargo.com.au; Thur–Sun noon–3pm, Tue–Sun 6–10.30pm; $$

Hidden in a quiet backstreet, the Argo is worth hunting out. A relaxed attitude is combined with meticulous attention to its modern European food, switched-on service and serious wine focus. The nicely refurbished venue has a landscaped courtyard with retractable roof and outdoor fireplace for those who want to chill out after dinner.

David's

4 Cecil Place, Prahran; tel: 9529 5199; www.davidsrestaurant.com.au; Mon–Fri noon–3pm, Sat–Sun 11.30am–3pm, Sun–Thur 6–10.30pm, Fri–Sat 6–11pm; $–$$

David's is one of the more adventurous and interesting Chinese restaurants in town, championing food from Shanghai and tea with health-giving properties. There are banquet menus available for two people or more, a *yum cha* (dim sum)

Price guide for a two-course dinner for one with a glass of house wine:

$$$$	over A$80
$$$	A$60–80
$$	A$45–60
$	below A$45

menu and an unusual array of tonic soups that (according to the restaurant) increase longevity and enhance libido and vitality. You can BYO; there is a corkage charge of A$10 per bottle for wine only.

Jacques Reymond

78 Williams Road, Windsor; tel: 9525 2178; www.jacquesreymond.com.au; Thur–Fri noon–1.30pm, Tue–Sat 6.30–9.30pm; $$$$

Vue de Monde may be more fashionable, but local epicures prefer the restrained elegance and sophisticated execution of Jacques Reymond's food, which he has been serving from this suburban mansion for decades. Don't let this long pedigree fool you, though – Reymond is still one of the most innovative and exciting chefs in Australia, and a meal here is extremely hard to beat.

Mama Ganoush

56 Chapel Street, Windsor; tel: 9521 4141; www.mamaganoush.com; Mon–Sat 6–10pm; $$

A visit to this chic restaurant at the southern end of Chapel Street is the local equivalent of a trip to the exotic souqs of Egypt and the Levant – with heady spices, bright colours and tasty treats on offer. Run by Melbourne's best-known Middle Eastern foodie family, it concentrates on Lebanese dishes with a modern twist and serves them with great exuberance.

St Kilda

Donovans

40 Jacka Boulevard; tel: 9534 8221; www.donovanshouse.com.au; daily noon–3pm, 6–10.30pm; $$$–$$$$

Resembling a chic Cape Cod beach cottage, Donovans combines bayside breeziness with an assured but conservative Italian menu heavy on seafood options. The views of St Kilda beach are fabulous and the 'cubby house' menu for kids is a great innovation.

Pizza e Birra

60a Fitzroy Street; tel: 9537 3465; www.pizzaebirra.com.au; Tue–Fri noon–3pm, Sun noon–4pm, Tue–Sat 6pm–late; $

The chef hails from Campania, so the pizzas served up here are of the thin-crust variety. They are a perfect match for the ice-cold beer provided on tap. Service is welcoming and the clientele is diverse, with families as much in evidence as glamorous 30-something professionals.

Stokehouse

30 Jacka Boulevard; tel: 9525 5555; www.stokehouse.com.au; daily noon–2pm and 6–10pm; $$–$$$$

This is one of the first ports of call when Melburnians want to impress visitors from out of town. The downstairs bar serves pizza and fish and chips, and the upstairs restaurant, which has a superb view of the bay, offers a progressive menu using the freshest ingredients.

Above from far left: Añada in Fitzroy; Stokehouse's beachside balcony.

Melbourne's bar scene is famous throughout Australia. Stylish drinking dens are located in obscure laneways throughout the city, and entertainment strips such as Brunswick, Gertrude and Chapel streets are full of edgy bars, pubs and clubs. For an overview of theatre, dance, music and film, *see pp.20–1*.

Central Melbourne

Bennetts Lane
25 Bennetts Lane; tel: 9663 2856; www.bennettslane.com; daily 8.30pm–late

The city's number-one jazz club, Bennetts Lane hosts local jazz luminaries and occasional high-profile international acts, such as Brad Mehldau. Though aficionados of the genre treat it like their local, it's an inclusive, attitude-free place.

The Carlton Hotel
Upstairs, 193 Bourke Street; tel: 9663 3216; www.thecarlton.com.au; Mon–Wed 3pm–late, Thur–Sun noon–late

Once a seedy pub with a depressing interior and rough-as-guts clientele, the Carlton has had a makeover and is now packing Generation Ys in every night. The witty decor, excellent wine list, tasty bar snacks, art exhibitions and boisterous vibe make it a general fave.

Gin Palace
10 Russell Place; tel: 9654 0533; www.ginpalace.com.au; daily 4pm–3am

The seductive strains of lounge music and sound of cocktail shakers getting a workout greet you on entering this Melbourne institution. Its velvet-upholstered lounge chairs are claimed by a predominantly 30-something crowd, who are devoted to the bar's expertly concocted Martinis.

Melbourne Supper Club
161 Spring Street; tel: 9654 6300; Sun–Mon 8pm–4am, Tue–Thur 5pm–4am, Fri 5pm–6am, Sat 8pm–6am

Everyone loves the Melbourne Supper Club. In winter chesterfields and armchairs in the first-floor bar beckon; in summer the views from the terrace Siglo bar are so wonderful that it's hard to leave at the end of the evening. The wine list is exceptional, there's great food and the service is exemplary. *See also p.36.*

Meyers Place
20 Meyers Place; tel: 9650 8609; Mon–Thur 4pm–1am, Fri–Sat 4pm–4am

One of the first laneway bars in Melbourne, Meyers Place was started by a group of architects who wanted a place where they and their boho friends could enjoy a quiet drink after work. Near Parliament House, it has been joined in the lane by the equally popular **Loop** (23 Meyers Place; tel: 9654 0500; www.looponline.com.au; daily 3pm–late).

Seamstress

113 Lonsdale Street; tel: 9663 6363; www.seamstress.com.au; Mon–Tue, Sat 6pm–1am, Wed–Fri 11pm–1am

It's hip, it's hot and it's most definitely happening. There's a restaurant and a cocktail bar, as well as Sweatshop, another bar in the basement. They are as stylish as they come and have quickly endeared themselves to the city's barflies. The owners know their wine and cocktails, and match these with a tempting array of bar snacks, including Chinese dumplings, freshly shucked oysters and crispy rice balls.

9521 5985; Mon–Thur noon–4am, Fri–Sun 24hr

Local and international DJs and bands take pride of place, but there are also record launches, indie film screenings and art exhibitions at this long-standing alternative venue. Check the website to see what's on.

St Kilda

George Lane Bar

1 George Lane (off Grey Street); tel: 9593 8884; www.georgelane bar.com.au; Wed–Fri 6pm–1am, Sat–Sun 7pm–1am

In a laneway behind the landmark George Hotel, this popular bar can't accommodate many drinkers, but those who do score a spot here always leave happy. There's a refreshingly laid-back vibe and a DJ at weekends. The nearby **George Public Bar** (located in the basement of the George Hotel, 127 Fitzroy Street; tel: 9534 8822) is a popular pool-and-a-pot place.

Fitzroy

Builder's Arms Hotel

211 Gertrude Street; tel: 9419 0818; Mon–Thur 4pm–late, Fri–Sun 2pm–late

There are bars along the length of Brunswick Street, but discerning drinkers prefer to make their way to nearby Gertrude Street, home to cutting-edge restaurants and down-to-earth drinking dens. The retro-themed Builder's Arms is the most popular of these, attracting a slightly older crowd and serving beer on tap, a decent array of house wine and exceptional Middle Eastern-accented pub grub.

Prahran, South Yarra and Toorak

Revolver Upstairs

229 Chapel Street, Prahran; www.revolverupstairs.com.au; tel:

Prince Bandroom

29 Fitzroy Street; tel: 9536 1168; www.princebandroom.com.au

One of Melbourne's most famous live-music venues, the Prince has a leafy balcony overlooking Fitzroy Street and an atmosphere-packed, somewhat rough downstairs bar. Acts are as diverse as the clientele, harking from both Australia and overseas, and have included Lenny Kravitz, Scissor Sisters, Pink, Coldplay and Bright Eyes.

CREDITS

Insight Step by Step Melbourne
Written by: Virginia Maxwell
Updated by: Amy Van
Commissioning Editor: Catherine Dreghorn
Series Editor: Carine Tracanelli
Picture Editor: Richard Cooke
Cartography by: APA Cartography Dept.
Map Production: Stephen Ramsay

Photography: All by APA/Jerry Dennis except:
APA/Glyn Genin 14TR, 17T; Axiom 2–3, 8–9;
Alamy 26–27, 30T; Dean Cambray 118; Cooee 24;
Mary Evans 24T; Fotolia 86–87; Getty 49B; John
Gollings 41; iStockphoto 11T, 34B, 40TR, 65T, 80,
81T, 85, 87TR; James Geer 13TR; Gil Meydan 32;
Photolibrary 35T, 36T; Mirek Rzadkowski 59; Tom
Smyth 91; Visions of Victoria 54T, 55B, 81B.
Front cover: main image: AWL Images; bottom
left and right: iStockphoto.

Printed by: CTPS – China

DISTRIBUTION

Worldwide
APA Publications GmbH & Co. Verlag KG
(Singapore branch)
7030 Ang Mo Kio Ave 5
08-65 Northstar @ AMK
Singapore 569880
Email: apasin@singnet.com.sg

UK and Ireland
Dorling Kindersley Ltd,
a Penguin Group company
80 Strand, London WC2R 0RL, UK
Email: customer.service@dk.com

United States
Ingram Publisher Services
One Ingram Blvd, PO Box 3006
La Vergne, TN 37086-1986
customer.service@ingrampublisherservices.com

Australia
Universal Publishers
PO Box 307
St Leonards, NSW 1590
Email: sales@universalpublishers.com.au

CONTACTING THE EDITORS

We would appreciate it if readers would alert us
to errors or outdated information by writing to
us at insight@apaguide.co.uk or APA Publications,
PO Box 7910, London SE1 1WE, UK.

www.insightguides.com

THE WORLD OF
INSIGHT GUIDES

Different people need different kinds of travel information. Some want background facts. Others seek personal recommendations. With a variety of different products – Insight Guides, Insight City Guides, Step by Step Guides, Smart Guides, Insight Fleximaps and our new Great Breaks series – we offer readers the perfect choice.

Insight Guides will turn your visit into an experience.

www.insightguides.com

INDEX

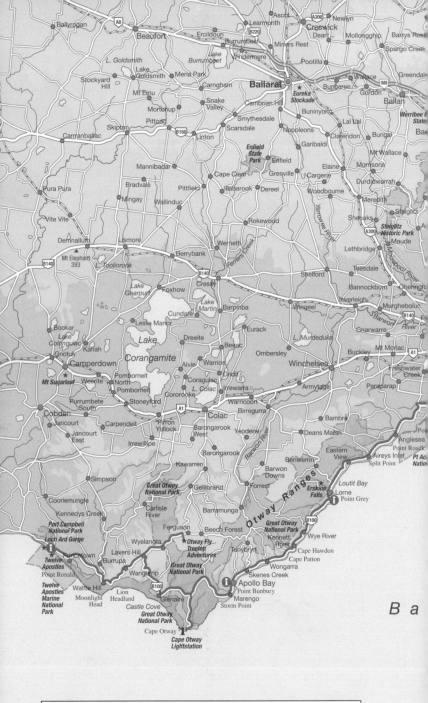

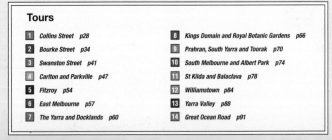

Mel▶

0
0